D0852927

IN SYSTEM

BUILDING A SUCCESSFUL

HOME STAGING

BUSINESS

BUILDING A SUCCESSFUL
HOME STAGING
BUSINESS

PROVEN STRATEGIES FROM THE
CREATOR OF HOME STAGING

BARB SCHWARZ

WITH MARY GOODBODY

BICENTENNIAL
1807
WILEY
2007
BICENTENNIAL

John Wiley & Sons, Inc.

Published by John Wiley & Sons, Inc., Hoboken, New Jersey.
Published simultaneously in Canada.

Wiley Bicentennial Logo: Richard J. Pacifico.

For general information on our other products and services or for technical support, please contact our Customer Care Department within the United States at (800) 762-2974, outside the United States at (317) 572-3993 or fax (317) 572-4002.

Wiley also publishes its books in a variety of electronic formats. Some content that appears in print may not be available in electronic books. For more information about Wiley products, visit our web site at www.wiley.com.

Library of Congress Cataloging-in-Publication Data:

Schwarz, Barb, 1944–
    Building a successful home staging business : proven strategies from the creator of home staging / Barb Schwarz.
        p. cm.
    ISBN 978-0-470-11935-8 (cloth)
    1. House selling.   2. Real estate business.   I. Title.
    HD1379.S3527   2006
    333.33'8068—dc22

                                                2007000459

Printed in the United States of America.

10 9 8 7 6 5 4 3 2 1

I dedicate my book to every ASP and ASPM who is now and is yet to be. It is you whom I thank and also look to for the future of Home Staging around the world. You are the now and all that is meant to be. In the years ahead, you will serve those in need of your services and extend your hands in care and kindness as you bring them your talent!
I believe in you.

You are the future of Home Staging and I give you my admiration and my love.

CONTENTS

BARB'S STAGING RESOURCE CENTER

ACKNOWLEDGMENTS

As I look back over my career and life, I realize there are thousands of people who have helped me along the way. If you are one of them, you know who you are and I thank you from the bottom of my heart and soul! I thank you for your belief in me, in my creation of Home Staging, and in my mission of sharing the good that it brings to people all around the world. The magic of Home Staging changes lives, and I thank you for being in my life and allowing me to come into yours!

The good in each of us resonates with the good in those around us. The creation of Home Staging, I now know, is a gift from God. This is my mission: to teach, share, and spread creativity for the utmost good of all whom I meet through the magic of Home Staging. Thank you all.

Special recognition goes to Debra Englander, my editor. Without you, this book would not exist in this way at this time. I thank you for your editorial expertise and recognize you as the leader you are in the publishing world. I remain dedicated to all those at John Wiley & Sons, who are likewise making a difference in the world of Home Staging through their belief in me and the power of Home Staging.

I give very special recognition to Mary Goodbody, whose help, support, writing talent, and patience I appreciate and am grateful for. Without you also, Mary, this book would not exist at this time in this special way. Thank you for your gift of writing and fine-tuning and the hours you spent going through my materials and courses with me to understand even better the world of Home Staging that I have created.

Thanks, too, to my agent, Jim McCarthy, who is with Dystel & Goderich Literary Management. Your hard work and belief in this project made all the difference. Thank you, Jim.

Barb Schwarz

BUILDING A SUCCESSFUL
HOME STAGING
BUSINESS

INTRODUCTION

Let us not strive to be people of success
but people of value
for when we are of value
to our companies, our clients,
and our communities,
then we shall be successful.
—INSPIRED BY ALBERT EINSTEIN'S QUOTATION:
"TRY NOT TO BECOME A MAN OF SUCCESS BUT
RATHER TO BECOME A MAN OF VALUE"

Destress the property and bring peace to it
with Home Staging.
—BARB SCHWARZ

Anyone who has met me knows one thing to be true: I believe passionately in Home Staging. It's my invention and my dream, and with the help of other Stagers with the same vision, I hope to change the world, one home and one family at a time. This book explains how to set up your own Home Staging business so that you can join the growing legions of creative men and women who are helping me change the way real estate is marketed and sold.

When you Stage a house or condominium, you are doing nothing more than marketing it so it can be sold to the highest bidder. It's that simple. In its purest sense, Staging is turning a home into a house, from which the sellers plan to get a high return.

Learning how to Stage means learning how to merchandise the product (the house). A well-Staged house allows the buyers to envision living in it. Buyers can mentally place their furniture in the rooms and let their minds wander to future happy times when the house has become their home.

When you learn how to Stage, you learn how to communicate with both the homeowners and the real estate agent. It's all about educating them so that they understand how certain changes will ensure financial rewards.

Staging is not decorating. When you decorate your home, you personalize it. When you Stage it, you do the opposite. In my classes I refer to the process as *depersonalizing,* which speaks volumes. You remove distractions so that potential buyers focus on the space, not what is in the space. The Staging professional must learn how to communicate with the homeowners so that they understand what should be done and never feel offended or hurt. No one wants to hear that their house is not clean or that it has an odor, but both problems will distract potential home buyers. It's the Home Stager's job to make the homeowners understand this and work to solve such problems.

Home Stagers rely on many skills, the two most important being their ability to communicate and their creativity. Without the former you will never win clients, and without the latter you won't Stage houses properly or effectively. I will address these and other issues in the chapters that follow.

MY EARLY STORY

I started Home Staging in 1972, when I coined the term *Staging* to refer to the process of preparing homes for sale. After teaching school for a few years and then running a small home decorating business in Bellevue, Washington, near Seattle, I rose to a real estate friend's challenge to become a real estate agent, too. "Why aren't you in real estate?" he asked me one day. Admittedly, I had thought about it now and then. I used to hold open houses for builders as an after-school and weekend job when I was in high school and I had always been interested in the business. When my friend asked the question, it sparked that dormant interest and literally changed my life.

When I first began, I was appalled by the appearance of many of my clients' houses. Some were filthy; others were crammed with knickknacks. Some were painted the most startlingly unattractive colors; others were falling apart at the seams. A few were all of the above! If you are in the real estate business, you know of what I speak. We've seen it all.

I didn't know how to tell the hopeful sellers that they needed to clean up their act. While I knew they didn't need or want to decorate, I didn't have the communication skills at that time to explain what needed to be done. I ended up treading on sensitive feelings, something I have always tried to avoid. During the first 18 months I was an agent, I found houses for many buyers and was named rookie of the year in the real estate office where I worked, but none of my own listings sold! I was distraught and knew I had to find a way to get past this roadblock.

I have always been musical and I love to perform. In my younger days, I flirted with being a professional singer or joining a musical theater company. Although I gave up pursuing a music career, I was still tuned in to the theater and started to view my real estate listings as sets that needed to be staged to attract buyers.

It struck me that potential home buyers glanced into rooms as they walked through a house, but unless they actually entered every one of them, they clearly were not interested in the house. How can you sell a property if the buyers don't invest time in every room, I asked? I realized that part of selling a property involves the same activity as putting on a play: You have to design the sets so that the audience is drawn into the drama. This was one of my first aha moments! I suggested to my clients that they set the stage for selling their houses, that they consider potential buyers the audience and real estate agents the critics for each other's listings.

The first client I shared this idea with was hesitant, but I knew she loved the theater. As I explained my concept, my enthusiasm grew with every sentence, and before long she warmed to the idea. She would be the producer and star, we decided, and I would be the director. It worked! Before I listed her property, it had been on the market with another company for several months. Once I Staged it, the house sold in a matter of days. Without really knowing how far-reaching that single event would be, I had indeed invented an industry: Home Staging. From that point on, I told every agent and seller I met that I Staged my listings and that once I did, they sold for top dollar. I sold many houses in the Seattle area that next year and was well on my way to becoming a successful real estate agent.

In 1985, a promoter for real estate seminars heard about my real estate business and how I Staged homes. He asked me to speak at a seminar. No one, the promoter said, had ever shared a concept like mine before. That was the beginning of my professional speaking career. Soon I was speaking for up to 40 weeks a year, presenting to real estate agents my ideas for Staging homes. I estimate that I addressed at least a million real estate agents during these years, and soon word began to spread. You can't talk to a million people and not expect your message to get out!

HOME STAGING TAKES CENTER STAGE

In 1998, I decided to go back to selling real estate in Seattle. I listened to an inner voice that urged me to "get off the road and back to the street." I knew this was the right thing to do for my family and for me, and in the end, it allowed me to be in one place so that I could launch my new real estate training/Staging business, StagedHomes.com.

In 2000, my world turned upside down. A gall bladder infection raged into a serious attack on some of my body's major organs and I went through two heart surgeries. To add insult to injury, I suffered a series of small strokes in one weekend.

Although I was unable to speak clearly for a while or move with much coordination, I did have a crystal clear vision of what I wanted to accomplish in the future: I wanted to train Home Stagers and real estate agents. This led to the creation of a certification program for the industry I had invented. Through this certification program, people earn the Accredited Staging Professional (ASP) designation. This was an important step toward ensuring that my industry would operate with a set of standards and ethics. I established the Staging University as a place of continuing education for anyone who becomes an ASP Stager.

Today there are 4,200 ASP Stagers who are spreading the good word about Home Staging—and their number grows every year. The ASP Stagers are building their businesses by serving others and doing what they love.

I also knew it was important to establish a professional association for networking and further education, and as a vehicle to reach the local communities where ASPs live and work. That association is the International Association of Home Staging Professionals (IAHSP). To learn more about it, visit www.IAHSP.com.

MY BUSINESS TODAY

From StagedHomes.com, I conduct training classes for Home Stagers and real estate agents. These two- and three-day courses, respectively, qualify participants as ASP Stagers or agents, or both. When they continue their education through the Staging University on our web site, they join the IAHSP and participate in a world-wide network of like-minded and trained Stagers and agents to serve the public in the best possible way.

With *Building a Successful Home Staging Business* in hand, you will learn what it takes to operate a thriving Staging business of your own. I wrote this book to give you an overview of what I have learned as I built the industry and to present specifics about starting and maintaining a Staging business. This book also offers you a taste of what I teach during the two- and three-day seminars. (This book is about building a Home Staging business. Although it offers a number of Staging ideas and tips, for a more detailed presentation, please refer to my previous book, *Home Staging: The Winning Way to Sell Your House for More Money,* John Wiley & Sons, 2006.)

Home Staging is growing by leaps and bounds, and as is the case with all young industries, the marketplace changes all the time. As useful as I believe this book to be, I hope it will stimulate you to visit StagedHomes.com and consider becoming an ASP Stager or ASP real estate agent. Our knowledge and continued support teamed with your enthusiasm and professionalism is a combination that can't be beat!

Welcome to the wonderful world of *Building a Successful Home Staging Business.* I look forward to sharing the journey with you!

CHAPTER 1

FROM THE BEGINNING

Staging is selling your space, not your things.
—BARB SCHWARZ

I started Staging houses and condominiums 35 years ago. At that time, I discovered what you will find today: It works!

For a good number of those years, I traveled around the country speaking to real estate professionals about the benefits of Home Staging. I estimate that I addressed more than a million people in those 14 years. You cannot speak to more than a million people and expect that the word won't get out! I believed wholeheartedly in my message and the need to convey it to real estate agents across the country. Because of this, the good news about Staging has spread. People are Staging houses from coast to coast. Television programs about selling real estate are often about Staging, whether the producers identify it as such or not. Magazine articles and web sites tout its benefits. Real estate agents suggest that their clients stage their properties, and with increasing frequency, sellers request that their houses be Staged.

All this is extremely gratifying to me, as I came up with the term decades ago when I developed the concept. Back then, I had no idea of the impact Staging would have on the real estate market, but recent years have shown that it has changed the real estate business forever.

WHY STAGE?

The most compelling reason sellers should agree to Stage their home is to get the best price for the property. Getting top dollar is a win-win situation for everyone involved: The homeowners can afford "more house" when they buy their next property, the real estate agent's commission is higher, and the Stager can add another successful job to the resume and a rewarding deposit to the bank account.

You might argue that the only people in the equation who do not win are the home buyers, but that's not so. Even they benefit because they have bought the house they want. The Staging enabled them to see exactly what they purchased, so there are no surprises come moving day. They also learn firsthand the value of Staging, which means that when they decide to sell they will be receptive to the idea and, in turn, will get a high price for the same house.

I get feedback from ecstatic sellers all the time. Recently, Sharon from Illinois wrote to tell me her Staged house had gone on the market on Wednesday. She said, "On Friday I had two offers for more than list price! Obviously, your service worked, despite skepticism from many family and friends, who all thought I was nuts." Or how about this from a seller who asked that I not use her name: "I told you I would let you know when we sold our house, so here I am. We sold it today. It was on the market for six days! I will enthusiastically recommend [Staging] to anyone I know selling a home."

I hear success stories from Stagers, as well. Two Stagers named Rahul and Melissa sent me an e-mail about a couple who had decided not to Stage because of the cost and because they had an active toddler. They assured their real estate agent that the house was "neat, very well kept." But it sat on the market for three months without a single offer. Then they called Rahul and Melissa for help. As they tell it, "While we were there helping hang pictures, rearrange furniture, and clean out the china cabinet, a real estate agent called and wanted to show the house right away. We worked furiously to Stage it and after only one and a half hours of work, they received three offers in two days."

The process of Home Staging is a never-ending circle—one that revolves around a desire to help people do the best they can with what, in most cases, is their most valuable asset. This is why I created Home Staging years ago—it was an act of love. And if you're uncomfortable with that idea, perhaps you should put down this book and think about another profession!

WHAT IS HOME STAGING?

During the more than 35 years that I have been in the real estate and Staging businesses, I have Staged and sold thousands of houses. When I started, I made every mistake in the book, but gradually I learned. Because I wanted to share what I knew with others in the business, I started teaching fellow real estate agents in greater Seattle, Washington, where I then lived. The idea slowly began to catch on, and today I am proud to say that with the concept of Staging, I am working to change the economy of real estate both in the United States and around the world.

Okay, okay. Enough about me! What is Home Staging? It is converting a home into a house that can be merchandised as a product. It is very much part of the real estate industry and not, as many believe, the decorating business. It's all about preparing the house for sale so that the client prospers.

Even so, Staging has nothing to do with the condition of the house. By this I mean that if the house needs a new roof or furnace or has a cracked foundation or sagging front porch, it needs more than Staging. These major concerns fall to the listing agent to discuss with the client. Once they are addressed, the house still needs to be Staged.

Staging is not decorating. Decorating is a way to personalize your living space, to announce to everyone who walks through the front door who you are and what you like. Staging is the opposite. It's the act of depersonalizing, taking the home out of the house without leaving it sterile or uninviting. It's the process of organizing any home inside and out so that buyers can see what they are getting and can, after a simple walk-through, start to imagine their family living inside those walls. If you keep in mind that when you decorate you are personalizing your home but when you Stage you are *de*personalizing it, you will never confuse the two.

WHY STAGING WORKS

Time and again I have witnessed a house that is not Staged sit on the market for months or even years and then, once it's been Staged, sell in days—and very often for the full asking price, or more.

Staging works because it allows buyers to see the house as it really is, without the distractions of the homeowner's clutter, collections, and, in some cases, extreme taste. A house shines when it is Staged. I mean this both literally and figuratively. Literally, the windows twinkle, the walls are free of scuff marks, the appliances and countertops sparkle, and the lamps glow warmly. A clean, clutterfree house welcomes everyone so that, regardless of the furniture, artwork, or color quirks, the buyers can really see what they are getting. The polish Stagers put on the property reassures the buyers about making the enormous financial commitment a house demands.

Trained Stagers create additional wealth for home sellers, which is why I always explain that Staging is an investment. And in nearly every case where trained Stagers are involved, it's an investment that pays off handsomely.

As I tell all the students who sign up for my three-day ASP Staging course, I experienced the benefits of Staging firsthand once again when I went back to selling real estate after 15 years away from it. During that time I had been a traveling speaker who addressed real estate agents around the country on the subject of Home Staging, but after all those years, I felt I had been called back to real estate. I have always found it best in life to follow my intuition; I have learned that if I don't, I run into brick walls. Long ago I gave up the fear that often accompanies decision making and determined to follow my instincts, and I did so this time, too. They led me directly into an industry that helps others—Home Staging. I urge you to do the same. Intuition is a gift from God, a sixth sense that links you to the energy in the universe.

It was 1998, the Seattle market was sound, and I was excited about getting back to the business of selling one-on-one. Nevertheless, the first house I listed had been on the market for 18 months and the second house had been on the market for four years. I Staged them both, and both of them sold to the first customers who saw them. Had I needed convincing that Staging still worked, those experiences would have done the job. Statistics prove that these two instances were not flukes.

STAGING STATISTICS

The way a house is prepared for sale is a significant factor in how much it sells for and how long it takes to sell. Independent studies as well as our own internal StagedHomes.com surveys confirm these assertions.

My company, StagedHomes.com, conducted a nationwide survey of houses Staged by ASPs during a two-year period between 2004 and 2006. About half of these houses were Staged before they went on the market and the rest were Staged *after* they had lingered without offers for an average of five and a half months (163.7 days). The results were remarkable and should convince any doubters to sit up and take notice.

The first group, the houses that were Staged before they were officially on the market, sold in 8.9 days on average, or three times faster than comparable new listings that were not Staged. They sold for an average of 100.3 percent of the asking price. In some markets, the houses sold for as much as 150 percent of the asking price, which in the high-end markets represented half a million dollars.

The second group, houses that had been sitting on the market for months before being Staged, sold in 13.7 days on average once Staged, or 13 times faster than otherwise. They sold for an average of 102 percent of the asking price, and like the houses in the first group, in some markets the percentage was as high as 150 percent. See Table 1.1 and Figure 1.1.

Table 1.1   Nationwide Trends and Staging Statistics

Type of Home	Average Days on Market	Average Days to Pending Status *after* Staging	Equity Increase
Homes Listed for Sale Prior to Staging These homes were not Staged for sale but were listed and did not sell. They then were Staged and sold quickly.	136 days (4.5 months)	7.6 days—up to 20 times faster than un-Staged homes!	3% minimum or $26,000 average (as much as 50% or $500,000 in some markets)
Homes Listed for Sale after Staging These homes were Staged and then listed for sale.	32–42 days (for un-Staged comparable homes)	6.8 days— 2 to 3 times faster than un-Staged homes.	3% minimum or $26,000 average (as much as 50% or $500,000 in some markets)

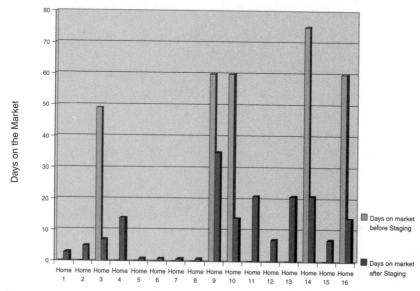

Figure 1.1 *Staging helps homes sell faster.* Some of the houses we surveyed had been sitting on the market for weeks or months.

STAGING SUCCESSES

Anecdotal evidence is even more impressive. The ASP Stagers I have trained frequently contact me with success stories, and every one of them warms my heart, even as it sustains my conviction that Staging is the most important change to come to real estate in generations.

Leigh Kendall-Lazarus, ASP, IAHSP, Staged a vacant house that had been on the market for seven months. After Staging, the house sold in three weeks for $530,000, the full asking price. Annie Pinsker-Brown, ASP, wrote me about a condominium in Reseda, California. "I did a very detailed consultation for the client and he did all the work," she said. The real estate agent told her the seller followed her recommendations to the letter, and the condo, which was, in Annie's words, "a real bachelor pad without any feminine touches," sold in the first five days on the market for $335,000. The list price? $324,000.

Jennie Norris, ASPM, deserves bragging rights because she

Staged a house that had been slated to be listed at $310,000. Once Jennie worked her Staging magic, the real estate agent raised the price to $317,000. There were five offers in five days, she says, and the house sold for $330,000. Jennie says the best part for her is that the agent is now singing her praises all over town and the sellers are "smiling all the way to the bank."

My student Donna Tanfani, ASP, sent me an e-mail saying that her client fired his first real estate agent. When he contracted with a new agent, that agent brought Donna on board. She Staged his vacant house, which by now had been on the market for more than two months, and it sold in 12 days. Both Donna and I raised our eyebrows in amazement when we heard that the first agent had told the homeowner that the house "did not need Staging."

Massachusetts broker Melissa Even told me about a property that had had 20 showings and five open houses for the public, but nary an offer. Melissa knew the price was right, so she decided to Stage the property. Success! Two of the first four parties to tour the house returned for a second visit, and one made an offer that was accepted. (The other interested party asked to be notified if the first deal fell through, and a third potential buyer asked to be apprised if the property came back on the market.)

THE ASP DESIGNATION

As you read in the introduction to this book, I had a vision for the Home Staging industry. I have realized my dream, and today the industry operates with a set of standards and a high level of professionalism. I have worked hard to bring my vision to fruition and create the Staging business. I did not want to see it grow in popularity without any controls to guarantee that homeowners would get their money's worth and that home buyers would be treated to a fair representation of what they were purchasing.

With my creation of the Accredited Staging Professional (ASP) designation, I am seeing my dream come true. Stagers and real estate agents who can add those three letters to their names are held in high regard throughout the industry.

The only way to earn the ASP designation—and the very best way to learn how to Stage—is to complete my three-day course. I teach the course, as do a group of superbly qualified trainers, through my company, StagedHomes.com. Upon completion of the course, students receive certification declaring them ASPs, which entitles them to use the designation after their name.

During the course, they learn the rudiments of Staging and get advice on setting up their own business. The three rigorous days consist of two and a half days of classroom instruction and a half day actually Staging a house for sale. After this training, the newly certified ASP Stagers are ready to take on the real estate market in their own regions.

But there's more. ASP Stagers are not sent from the classroom back to their home towns without ongoing support. StagedHomes .com offers help at every turn. This means that not only do the Stagers gain knowledge, skills, and personal empowerment from the ASP class, but they also have access to all that the company offers. These are some of the benefits:

- An ASP certificate at course completion.
- A copy of the ASP Stager manual and ASP Stager supplemental materials.
- An ASP Stager Career Book and Career Book DVD or video.
- The ASP Stager Marketing Portfolio.
- An ASP Marketing CD album.
- My DVDs (or videos) *How to Stage Your Home to Sell for Top Dollar!* and *How to Price Your Home to Sell for Top Dollar!*
- An ASP apron and ASP lapel pin.
- An information listing about themselves posted on the StagedHomes.com web site.

- Access to the web site where Stagers can post pictures of the houses they have Staged.
- Their own ASP feature page on the StagedHomes.com web site.
- Access to Staging University (more on this later).
- Permission to use the licensed Stage trademark.
- A one-year membership in the International Association of Home Staging Professionals (IAHSP).
- ASP continuing education courses as long as they remain ASP members in good standing.
- My best-selling book *Home Staging: The Winning Way to Sell Your House for More Money.*

ASP Stagers can easily further their education and attain an ASPM, which is a master's designation in Staging. To achieve this level, in addition to the ASP Stager course, they must complete a five-day, hands-on course working in the field with me. This intense period of instruction incorporates the latest ideas for marketing and building your business, as well as the most up-to-the-minute tips I have developed for Staging houses. We also go shopping to preview the newest Staging accessories and supplies. The Master's course requires students to prepare and present a bid and a consultation to me in front of other students, which I then critique. This is extremely beneficial because the students must learn to communicate more effectively. And, of course, good communication skills are key to becoming a top producer.

Real estate agents, too, can earn an ASP designation by attending the first two days of the Stagers' three-day course. This means the real estate agent invests half a day in Staging a house that is poised to go on the market. Real estate agents who earn the ASP real estate agent designation can help homeowners properly prepare their houses for sale and, most important, sell the houses quickly and profitably. These agents realize the value of Staging when they see it up close and experience it in action.

STAGING UNIVERSITY

I believe that education is all-important. I started my adult life as a schoolteacher, and although I moved into other fields, teaching has always been in my blood. For this reason, I founded and have expanded the Staging University, which is the only such institution of its kind. All ASP Stagers and ASP real estate agents have the opportunity to continue their education at the StagedHomes.com university.

Staging University is a rich resource for all ASPs. Their clients benefit, too, because the ASPs have access to the most up-to-date materials, forms, and education available anywhere. ASPs post Staging ideas on the university web site, as do I and my staff.

Becoming an ASP entitles you to read the latest issue of our monthly ezine, "B Stage," download important legal and business forms, and surf through page upon page of before-and-after photographs. As you browse the online university, you will find new information with every click of the mouse, and you can count on my staff and me to update this information constantly. Staging University is a vital part of keeping the Home Staging industry on the cutting edge.

THE INTERNATIONAL ASSOCIATION OF HOME STAGING PROFESSIONALS

Everyone who qualifies as an ASP is automatically eligible to become a member of the International Association of Staging Professionals (IAHSP). Membership is renewable annually, and once you join, I am sure you will want to continue to belong. Why? Because IAHSP is all about community. It serves the needs of ASPs, just as ASPs serve the needs of the communities where they live and work.

Membership in the IAHSP enables you to participate in regional chapters with fellow ASP Stagers and ASP real estate agents, which is a wonderful networking opportunity. You will receive the monthly newsletter, and you can participate in organized conference calls with other Stagers.

Opportunities for marketing are considerable with IAHSP membership. You can use the ASP logos; you can take advantage of relationships with companies such as PODS, 1-800-Got-Junk, and Linens-N-Things; and you will have access to a low-interest credit card. These benefits can be a big help to your clients, who tend to be cash poor while they are selling their property and buying a new one.

Perhaps the best benefit is that as an IAHSP member, you have access to your own featured page on which to showcase your Home Staging business. This featured page is your personal advertisement, telling visitors who you are, what you do, and why you are the best. Business will be driven from our web site to yours. The content of this page is yours to develop, although we will transfer the content from your ASP featured page to your IAHSP home page for you.

Once a year, the IAHSP Foundation, our charitable organization, hosts Staging Service Week, during which regional chapters get together and donate their time to Stage a public space as a way to serve their communities. This might be a shelter, a day care center, a hospice facility, or, as one chapter recently did, a Ronald McDonald House. Because Staging brings peace to a property, this process improves the environment for everyone involved with the Staged locale. Not only does this bring joy and beauty to a small corner of the world, it also brings Stagers together, in spirit and love, to accomplish something meaningful. ASPs contribute their time, talent, skills, and dollars in the service of others to share the gift of Staging.

PROFESSIONAL POLICIES

No one will be surprised to hear that some folks don't take Staging seriously—or at least not until they learn about its results. To head these skeptics off at the pass, I can't emphasize enough how important it is to conduct yourself professionally as a Home Stager. Once you earn the ASP designation, it's imperative that you establish your own set of professional policies and let your clients know what they are.

I have my own policies and I am happy to share them with any ASP Stager. Yours may be similar to mine or they may be quite different, but as a rule they clearly state how you work and should be part of your written material, easily available to homeowners.

Your professional policies will establish the nuts and bolts of your business: what days you are available, when and how you can be reached by telephone or e-mail, whether you put up signs on the property announcing that it is being Staged, how you charge, and so forth.

Notice I said that the policies should state how you charge, but they not do list the fees. Those should be tailored to the particular job, although your policies will explain when you set your fees and how you go about figuring them. (Much more about this is in Chapter 6.)

I also expect all ASP Stagers and real estate agents to abide by the ASP Code of Ethics:

- I believe in my ability to help my clients Stage their properties.
- I will follow and protect this Code of Ethics for all Accredited Staging Professionals (ASPs).
- I will establish and maintain professional policies to hold my clients accountable to prepare their homes for sale and keep them in Staged showing condition until the home is sold and the inspection and appraisal are completed.
- I will protect the quality of Staging by following the Staging Criteria and only using the word "Staged" to describe homes that have truly met or exceeded those criteria.

- I will protect the Stage® trademark by including the registered trademark symbol (®) with any derivation of the word in any print advertising or marketing that I do.
- I will protect the Accredited Staging Professional™ trademark by including the trademark symbol (™) with any marketing or print advertising that I do with the ASP™ designation.
- I will honor the Staging University by not releasing my password to the university to anyone who is not an ASP member.
- I will display and market my ASP designation in my Staging marketing materials to inform people that I am an Accredited Staging Professional.
- I will educate my clients and the public as to the meaning and origin of Staging to enhance the ASP designation for all ASPs.
- I will bring credit to the ASP designation through my honesty, my integrity, and by honoring my clients and myself.
- I will honor all ASPs with the dignity and the respect of the designation for the greater good of all.

CHAPTER 2
STARTING YOUR HOME STAGING BUSINESS

As Stagers, we make magic happen!
—BARB SCHWARZ

Are you thinking about starting a Home Staging business? Do you already have one and want to see it grow? You are in luck! Not only do I have winning strategies for making your dreams come true, but the concept of Staging is catching on like wildfire from the Pacific to the Atlantic, and beyond. I have trained Stagers who live in countries as far-flung as Romania and Japan.

Home Staging is a relatively young industry, so, by definition, it attracts ambitious, energetic people who see all sorts of possibilities by getting in on the ground floor. I have been Staging houses and lecturing about it to real estate professionals for the past 35 years, but it's an idea that only recently has come into its own.

I could not be happier! It's my greatest pleasure to see creative, lively people succeed as Stagers and discover the joy that Staging brings.

ALWAYS ROOM FOR ONE MORE

There are 2.2 million licensed real estate agents in the United States and currently only 4,200 ASP Stagers. You do the math! Real estate agents need Stagers to help them sell their listings, and homeowners need them to show their property off to its best advantage.

I predict that in the next few years, Staging will become as important to real estate as are home inspections and open houses. Whether the market is hot or stone-cold, houses will always need to be bought and sold, and Staging has proven to move houses quickly and profitably. This is a business without boundaries. It will never go out of fashion or be overtaken by some sort of technology.

Just as any market does, the real estate market will wax and wane, but it will never die. We all have to live somewhere and we all will, on occasion, need to move. For many of us, our houses or condominiums are our biggest financial asset and so when it's time to sell one property and move on to the next, it's critical that we maximize this asset. Enter the ASP-trained Home Stager to help the homeowner and real estate professional do just that.

Best of all, Staging is an exciting and gratifying career. By relying on your own creativity and get-up-and-go, you will earn good money and go home every night feeling good about yourself. When you successfully Stage a home, you help people who have decided to sell their house realize their financial worth, and you help buyers see their investment with no hidden surprises.

I can't think of a better way to make a living.

Many others agree. For example, Cindy Lin, ASP, IAHSP, told me about her business, Staged4more Home Staging Services with these uplifting words: "Little did I know you would change my life when I heard you speak at the National Association of Realtors Conference in San Francisco. But you did," she wrote in an e-mail. "Soon after the conference, I started my own Staging company and now love being my own boss. It feels great to see the total transformation once I Stage the sellers' home and help them move on to the next stage of their lives. I also love to help clients declutter their homes so that they feel more at ease living in them. It is incredibly rewarding to have such a life-transforming job. The possibilities for Staging are endless, and as you always say, 'I love this business!' Even as it challenges my weaknesses, such as reaching out for new business and marketing, it exercises my creativity.

"Furthermore, Staging works! Here in the Bay Area, houses usually sit on the market for at least 40 days, but recently I Staged a house that sold two days later at the sellers' first open house! I was shocked when the real estate agent called me with news of the sale. I am happy with how my small business is growing and I am excited about what the future holds. And I owe it all to you."

SET YOUR GOALS

Goals are important when you start your own business. I like to say that a goal is a dream with a date on it.

To identify your goals, make a plan. I am not talking about a business plan, although that is very important (I will discuss business plans at length in Chapter 3). Here, I refer to your goals for the business.

When you write your goals, think about the time span you allot to each one. Is this an immediate goal (next week)? A short-term goal (in the next six months)? A midterm goal (next year)? Or a long-term goal (the next two to five years)?

Sit down with a pencil and paper or at the computer and list all you hope to achieve with your Staging business and, as I said, look at both long- and short-term goals. Once you have jotted down a laundry list of ideas, walk away. Go for a run or cook dinner for the kids and come back to the list the next day. Reassess your goals and discard those that do not seem relevant.

Examples of goals might be:

- I want to gross $X in the first quarter, $X by midyear, and $X by year's end.
- I want to double this income, within three years.
- I want to make money to pay for our family's health insurance (mortgage, private school, annual vacation).
- I want to work only in the mornings and be home for the kids in the afternoons.
- I want to work only on weekends.
- I would like to work as much as I possibly can.
- I want to work as many hours as I can. I want to work with a variety of realtors.
- I want to work with a business partner.
- I want my spouse, my friend, or a significant other to be a part of my business.
- I want to create a business that my children can join when they become ASP Stagers in the future.
- I want to work with other ASP Stagers whenever possible.
- I want to put together a top-notch Staging team.
- I want to be a profitable entrepreneur.
- I want to satisfy my desire to be creative.
- I want to help my neighbors and fellow townspeople make our community the best it can be.
- I eventually want to quit my current job and concentrate only on Staging.
- I want to be the biggest and best ASP Stager in the state.
- I want to be totally self-sufficient and own a thriving business.
- I want to run a small business that makes enough money to keep me profitable.
- I want to earn large sums of money.
- I want to serve humankind and be in the service of others.

As you can see from this list, when you first write down your goals, they could be all over the place. It's important to commit them to paper, since just the process of figuring out how to articulate them helps you shape your business.

Over time, your goals may very well change. Plan to revisit the list every few months while you are building your business to help you stay on track. Over the years, visit the list again and judge how many goals you have met. Edit the list, and add new goals. This will keep your business fresh. I will discuss other ways to keep the business innovative in later chapters, but my underlying message is that although running your own business is a joyous experience, you have to tend to it constantly to keep it growing and prospering.

Once you have a concrete list of goals, prioritize them in order of importance to you. From here, it will be an easy matter to write your mission statement, which I will expound on in Chapter 3, and from the mission statement you will create a business plan. All businesses are webs of ideas that intersect with each other—and a Home Staging business is no different. Because of this, it's gratifying to know that your goals lead directly to something as ultimately valuable as your mission statement and business plan.

THE FIVE KEYS TO YOUR SUCCESS

You could be the greatest Stager in the world, but if your attitude, marketing and business skills, and ability to communicate are not first-rate, your business will wither on the vine. I am here to make sure that does not happen!

So many variables contribute to a successful business that it's not easy to quantify them, but I have identified five keys to success. During the years I have been in business and taught others how to build successful Staging companies, I have identified these as attitude, business expertise, marketing proficiency, Staging skills, and communication.

As you read through this book, these five elements will be addressed over and over, with a lot of explanation on how to achieve them. Before you read any further, I will crystallize them for you.

1. *Attitude.* When I wake up every morning I can hardly wait to find out what that day will bring. I bring this enthusiasm with me to my work and while it may sound obvious or even of minor importance, I can't stress how crucial a positive, upbeat attitude is. Think of every day as an opportunity to enlighten real estate professionals and homeowners about Staging. When you do, your business will flourish and grow. Make a priority list of things to do and people to contact. I can't tell you how many times I have heard "no" during my career, but with the right attitude, I quickly learned that every "no" is just one step closer to "yes!"

2. *Marketing.* You must market your business to two primary outlets: the real estate community and the public. There are numerous ways to structure a marketing plan, as I discuss in Chapter 7. Once you have a plan in place, the challenge is to keep it vibrant and lively. Target your market as narrowly as makes sense and get out into the community and meet as many people as you can face-to-face. Soon, you will recognize marketing opportunities as they come along. As I always say, the world is full of money; find some!

3. *Business expertise.* As well as comporting yourself professionally, you need to have business skills that include computer competence; organizational abilities; knowing how and when to hire full-time, part-time, or freelance employees; and fundamental bookkeeping capabilities (plus the good sense to work with an accountant and tax advisor). The most significant business decision you can make when you establish your company is to buy liability insurance.

Read Chapter 4 for more information on this and other nuts-and-bolts aspects of setting up the business. Read Chapters 3 and 6 for more on establishing the road map and setting fees for your business.

4. *Staging skills.* Without question I could write dozens of books about how to Stage properties for success. Take your craft seriously and keep it fresh, fresh, fresh! You never want to hear a real estate agent comment that you Stage "the same way every time." Remember that you represent the person who pays you, which usually is the homeowner, and a good part of your Staging ability is how you meet his or her expectations. I predict a paradigm shift in who pays for Staging, with real estate agents soon including it as part of their marketing plans. At the same time, homeowners are starting to contact Stagers directly, bypassing the real estate agent altogether. Regardless, keep telling yourself you are "a creative genius, an artist, and someone who Stages homes artistically." Not only is this *true,* but if you have any doubts, they soon will disappear like mist before the sun.

5. *Communication.* Perhaps this should be the number one key to success. How you communicate with your clients and the real estate community spells success and you might say is the key to the kingdom. Clients need to be educated. They must understand that how they live in their home is very different from how they sell their house. Staging represents temporary changes that remove the home from the house and create a product. I discuss this in more detail in Chapter 5 and throughout the book, but how you communicate with the seller and how you demonstrate your kind and gentle human side make all the difference. If the homeowners are reluctant to stage the property, either they are not ready to sell or the Stager has not explained Staging clearly enough. You can't do much about the former, but you can absolutely remedy the latter.

BARB'S CHECKLIST FOR GETTING STARTED

You have decided to take the plunge and open your own business. Good for you! I have come up with a checklist of 12 things you should do to get going. Some will seem obvious; all are important.

1. *Name your business.* When you give your business a name, you will feel committed and enthusiastic about the new venture. Choose a name that says exactly what you do. This will make it easy for people to recognize what services you offer. Be sure the name is broad enough so that you can easily expand your services as time goes by.

    Here are a few examples of the names our ASP Stagers have selected. I am constantly amazed by the cleverness and ingenuity of our members!

    Setting the Stage

    Forsythe Home Staging

    IMPACT! Home Staging

    Real Estate Staging Services

    Staging My Home

    Refreshing Space

    Stage and Sell

2. *Talk to your accountant.* Decide if you should be a sole proprietor, a partnership, or a corporation. Once you decide, register your business with your local municipality and state. Local laws, regulations, and fees change all the time, so before you register your company, take the time to investigate the forms you will need. Start with the city office or town clerk and go from there. Local chambers of commerce are helpful, too. If you know people in the real estate business, bend their ear. Spend some time on the state's official web site for agencies that sound as though they could be

helpful to start-up businesses, or look for the state's small business administration web site.

This is one of those important steps that could spell success, or not. When you register your business and apply for a business license, you are stating that you own the name of the company. At the same time, you could discover that there is another company of the same name in your area. This is not permitted, of course, so the very act of applying for a business license eases your mind that your business name is yours and yours alone, and no one is going to come after you for infringement.

It's a happy day when your business license arrives and you can honestly begin to say: "I'm in business!"

3. *Decide on your business address.* Post office numbers and apartment numbers raise concerns with some customers, who feel that a business is more legitimate if it has a bricks-and-mortar base of operation with a street address. You may be setting up a home-based business. If using your street address concerns you, leave it off your business correspondence. If you live in an apartment or condominium, you can switch the word "apartment" to "suite"; the postal deliveryperson will understand. As I've indicated, many ASP Stagers simply put their e-mail address and telephone contact information on their business cards and stationery and leave off the street address. If you need to give a client or business associate your address later, you can make the decision on a case-by-case basis. You could also get a second set of cards printed with your address for these folks.

4. *Open a commercial checking account.* This is just good business practice. Do not commingle your personal and business funds! Put your company name, business address, e-mail address, and telephone number on the checks. This is not the place to be guarded about your address. When you write checks in stores, the clerk will want to match

your street address to your driver's license. Ask for the highest start number on the checks the bank allows so that your early vendors won't suspect they are working with a rank beginner. Use these checks for every business expense; this way, you will always have a record.

5. *Get a telephone number equipped with voice mail or buy a telephone with an answering machine.* It's best to have a separate commercial line installed in your house if you work out of a home office. Although you will save money if you rely on your residential line, with a commercial line, you will be listed in the Yellow Pages. Plus there's less chance that little Johnnie will answer the phone just when Mr. or Ms. Very Important Client calls!

   Sign up, too, with a good cell phone service provider. It's crucial that you can be reached when you are out working, and a reliable cell phone will save you a lot of headaches. In my experience, you get what you pay for with cell phones, and it does not pay to cut too many corners. While you do not need the top-of-the-line phone, don't buy the cut-rate one, either.

6. *Set your fees.* There is a difference between your fee and your hourly rate. The former is what you charge, the latter is for add-on work only. This may surprise you, and I will talk more about it in Chapter 6. Still, it's crucial that you know your hourly rate before you hang your shingle, so that you are clear about how much you will charge for a single hour of work, or what I call add-on work. Do not undervalue yourself, but do not price yourself out of the market. You can raise or lower your rates down the road. Markets fluctuate, and each house is different. No two houses are handled the same way, even if they have the same floor plan. The more junk and clutter, the bigger the Staging project. And remember, this is *your* business. You

can always adjust your fees. As you will see later in this book, I suggest that you quote prices on a project-by-project basis and not simply by the hour. But we will get into this in far more detail in Chapter 6.

7. *Purchase business/liability insurance now!* This is essential, as I will explain in Chapter 4. No one should be Staging homes without it. Call and discuss business insurance with your insurance broker, and don't be afraid to shop around.

8. *Stock your office and check your equipment.* Do not waste money on items you don't need (and I know as well as anyone how seductive big office supply stores can be), but make sure you have enough basic supplies such as folders, paper clips, tape, pens, legal pads, and stamps.

    Upgrade you computer, if need be, so that it can handle high-resolution digital photo files. Buy a very good digital camera capable of taking high-resolution photographs. Learn how to download photos onto the computer. You will use the camera over and over as you work, and you will discover it is among your prized possessions. You may find it helpful to have two cameras and extra batteries for both. (You might forget to charge the camera just when you get a call from a potential client.)

9. *Create letterhead and business cards on your computer.* If you cannot or don't want to do this yourself, order both from a local stationery or copy shop. ASP Stagers can go to my web site, StagedHomes.com, to review the marketing materials we provide for them and that they can use in their business. Make sure the business card contains your business phone number and cell phone number and includes your e-mail address. You will need one box of letterheads and 500 business cards to start. I also suggest having number 10 envelopes (business size) printed with your return address. If not, you can order a rubber stamp with your

address for envelopes—but I think you will agree that it looks far more professional to have the address printed on your envelopes.

10. *Identify local resources that will be helpful and send business your way.* Contact the local chamber of commerce and real estate organizations; see if you can join the latter as an affiliate. Other possibilities are Rotary Clubs, Welcome Wagon, and women's clubs. I highly recommend that you join Toastmasters International so that you learn how to make presentations in front of real estate companies and other groups.

    Visit the local library and scour any registries that list local business organizations. Read books about running a small business and about real estate. Knowledge is never wasted. Look for a mentor.

11. *Authorize and sign the ASP Stage License agreement with StagedHomes.com and join the International Association of Home Staging Professionals (IAHSP).* You will find all the information you need to run your business on our web site. As you read in Chapter 1, Stagedhomes.com offers ongoing support, and once you have earned your ASP certification, you will be able to take advantage of all of it.

12. *Invest time on our web sites, StagedHomes.com and iahsp.com.* You will learn a lot by reading about your fellow members, from our newsletter, and from the pages of information. When you become an ASP Stager, download all the PDF files from the Staging University found on our web site. The more time you invest in the university pages, the more you will learn and the better you will be able to serve your clients.

Once you have your licenses in hand, your business cards printed, and your office in order, you are ready to begin your career as a Home Stager. If you are not an ASP Stager, I urge you to visit

StagedHomes.com to see when we're next holding an ASP training session. Taking my class and getting your ASP designation is a big first step to a successful Staging business.

Even once you become an ASP Stager and after you've completed all of the 12 steps, there is more to do. One of those things is to create a business plan. Read on!

CHAPTER 3

YOUR BUSINESS PLAN

The investment of Staging *in* your home is
less than a price reduction *on* your home.
—BARB SCHWARZ

Once you create a good business plan, you will be ready to go. If you are anything like me, you are most excited about getting down to the business of helping homeowners Stage their properties, as you give free rein to your creativity. Despite my eagerness to get going, I have the utmost respect for careful planning, and this includes writing a comprehensive business plan. A business plan is an important part of the process of getting your business off the ground.

You may have read books, worked with other Stagers, sold real estate, or taken my ASP Staging course, but without a business plan, your fledgling Staging business may never take off. Regardless of how confident you feel, how well connected you are, or how creative you know yourself to be, you owe it to yourself and your future clients to do it right. A straightforward business plan will propel you toward success more assuredly than anything else.

Writing a business plan will ensure that you invest productive time doing what is necessary to create revenue for your business. A clear and concise business plan helps delineate the difference between being busy and running a business. As you know, the former is the "stuff" that occupies our time and tricks us into feeling productive, while the latter is what we do to make the engine of our Staging business run smoothly and profitably.

There is a big difference between being busy and being productive. When people ask me how I am doing or how things are going, I answer truthfully, "I have never been more productive in my life—some people are busy, but I am being really productive these days, and it feels great!"

The real trick is finding a balance between busyness and good business. This is where the business plan comes in. A business plan is composed of five elements:

1. Your mission statement.
2. Your goals.
3. Your target markets.
4. Your daily activities.
5. Details, details, details.

THE MISSION STATEMENT

Every business and every organization should have a mission statement. It defines, in just a few sentences, why the business exists and what it hopes to accomplish. Invest as much time as you need in writing the mission statement—once you get it right, it will ground you as nothing else can. When you have a bad day or feel untethered from your business, pull out the mission statement and read it. You will come right back to where you began, and it will reassure you.

We burn out when we lose sight of our mission. I am on a mission to Stage the world. I believe that through the magic of Home Staging we can bring peace to our environments and in turn to those who occupy these spaces. Selling a Staged home or living in a Staged home is a calm and nearly stressfree experience.

The mission statement is the cornerstone of your business *plan* and, thus, of your business. Before you write the plan, define your mission. In Hollywood, they call this the "high concept"—the few words that convey an idea so that everyone gets it.

Keep in mind that every successful business provides solutions for its clients. A computer company helps you understand which hardware or software will make your life better; a lawn service relieves you of the worry of an unkempt yard; an airline makes it possible for you to get from point A to point B; a plumber ensures that you can take a hot shower. An ASP Home Stager helps homeowners sell their houses or condominiums. Keep this in mind when you write your mission statement.

The mission statement for your Staging business might read as follows:

> To professionally prepare homes for sale by providing excellent Home Staging services to real estate agents and sellers. As I do so, I will apply my best Staging techniques and rely on my personal integrity and honesty to get the job done for my clients. I will rely on the skill sets learned in my ASP training and remain true to the ASP Code of Ethics.

Look back at the list of goals you prepared, as discussed in Chapter 2. They should help you formulate answers to the following questions:

- What kind of business do I want?
- What am I most passionate about when I think of my business?
- What values are most important to me? (These could include honesty, integrity, diversity, and creativity, for example.)

Ask a friend to take notes while you explain why you want to start your business. The key words that come pouring out of you should give you a good idea about what your mission statement should say, which boils down to stating your purpose. I consider them to be one and the same: My mission is my purpose, and my business is my life.

When you are ready to create your mission statement, use as few words as you can to write it, keeping the sentences short and clear. Some mission statements are no more than a single, concise sentence. The words your friend writes down for you should appear in the mission statement, and in no time everything will come together.

The mission statement will head your longer business plan, so there is no reason to include anything more than the essentials in it. *Stage* your ideas and distill them to their essence: You now have a mission statement. Congratulations!

The mission statement (like careful Home Staging) sets the stage for the larger purpose: the business plan (or in the case of Home Staging, the sale of the property). It is what will make your company come alive to you and your clients. It's a short descriptor of who you are, what your purpose is and what you want to do, and how you will do it. As concise as you make it, it should nevertheless convey passion for what you hope to accomplish.

Here is my mission statement:

Training One Person at a Time, Staging One Home at a Time, and Empowering One Family At a Time Through the Magic of Home Staging. I am dedicated to change what worked yesterday for what excels today, and that which opens the way to tomorrow through the world of Home Staging and Training at StagedHomes.com! by Barb Schwarz

YOUR GOALS, YOUR ROAD MAP

I have referred to the *business plan* several times in this chapter, but I confess that I prefer the term *road map*. *Road map* defines exactly what a business plan is: a guide to finding your way to the goals you have set for your business. You wouldn't leave on a long automobile trip without a map; you should not embark on a new business venture without one, either. The sad truth is that some people spend more time planning a road trip than they do investing in their business. Don't fall into this trap. I often say: If you fail to plan, you may inadvertently plan to fail.

One of my students sent me a lovely note about the value of preparing herself for the business. "I had to muster up the courage to take an ASP class," she said, explaining that she is Korean and believes her English is not very good. But she persevered, even though she said she made a lot of mistakes "because of the language barrier." Today, she wrote, she has been Staging for six months. "Most of my clients are not Korean. I surely can say the language is not a big problem. I have confidence and I try to develop my skills all the time. I have a dream to open a Staged Homes business in Korea and [give] Staging classes for the Korean community here. I am now taking your ASPM class." This wonderful woman, Jasmin Min, ASPM, exemplifies the point that with careful planning and a confident spirit, you can launch a successful business.

A business plan can be many pages long, or it can be far shorter. It's a living document that will evolve as your business does, and yet it's only as strong as its foundation. The plan should include your short-, mid-, and long-range goals, your targeted markets, your daily commitments to how you will operate your business, and a financial plan. I will discuss how to develop a financial plan in Chapter 6.

IDENTIFY YOUR MARKET AND WHO YOU WANT TO TARGET

The market you are after can include as large a geographical area as you like. Some of us live in sparsely populated regions of the country and are used to driving long distances. These people would not feel the least hesitation about traveling for an hour to Stage a house. Many others of us live in congested suburban areas and therefore find our Staging jobs closer to home.

The choice is yours, but my attitude has always been that if they call me, I will go. I don't care how far away the client is. If I have to charge a travel fee and the homeowner still wants to work with me, then why not? I go where I am called because I love to Stage.

Defining your market is about a lot more than geography, however. Decide which businesses, people, or segments of a market you plan to work with. This is a crucial issue that you need to address. You might want to Stage private homes only, or you might want to venture into public spaces. You may want to Stage very large houses, or, conversely, you may want to Stage in the condominium market. The senior market needs you; builders need you; vacant homes need you. The choice is yours. It is your business. The field is wide open.

Be specific as you define your target markets in your business plan. You can always adjust them, but it helps to know what sector of the real estate market challenges you the most. Break these down into major target markets and then into submarkets.

DAILY ACTIVITIES THAT BRING IT ALL TO LIFE

When you start a business, you make a commitment to work at it every day. This is not to say you can't take weekends off or drive your child to summer camp, but the difference between a business and a hobby is that the former is a serious commitment meant to serve people and generate revenue, while the latter activities are usually for fun and may not generate revenue. (Of course, Staging houses is fun, too, so you are way ahead of the game when you become an ASP Stager, as you get to have a good time while you make money.)

What you do each day drives your business. Therefore, it's helpful to include an explanation of your daily activities in your business plan. *Action* is a potent word, and when executed, an even better tool. *Act on it* and make it happen, I always say.

I am known as the "Do It Now Woman." Maintaining a "Do It Now" attitude moves us along much more effectively than getting stuck at the planning stage and letting weeks go by before taking action. Action is the key to daily tasks. When you feel down, simply taking immediate action makes you feel better, regardless of what is making you despondent. Action is powerful because it puts energy into motion, and once that starts, nearly any situation turns around for the better.

I heard from beginning Stager Kristy Love, ASP, who put the idea of completing daily tasks to the test after taking an ASP training course in Arizona. "I think I'm still in shock that this opportunity is no longer a dream," she wrote. "I already have two appointments today with real estate agents and I am shaking with excitement. All the 'no's' in world wouldn't hold me back at this point. [I feel that] this is the beginning of the most incredible journey for me." Good for you, Kristy! You are taking action, and proceeding action by action takes us to where we want to be—and even further!

Think about the days you will work, and be honest about how much you are willing to do to drive your business forward and achieve your goals. For instance, you might decide that every day you will make X number of personal contacts, send X number of e-mails, and make X number of telephone calls. You might decide that weekly or monthly you will make X number of presentations to real estate companies, X number of appointments with individual agents, and X number of appointments with real estate company owners or sales managers.

These plans ensure that the weeks and days are committed, and you have something to hold yourself accountable for each day. Commitment comes first, followed by accountability. To illustrate this, draw a triangle. At the lower left corner write *commitment;* at the lower right corner write *accountability;* in the middle of the triangle write *action;* at the top of the triangle write *results.* Commitment, accountability, and action all come together to produce results. It works!

These are small gestures in and of themselves, but it's easy to see how quickly they come together to push your business in the right direction. Writing them down in your business plan is a good way to turn your dream into a business.

DETAILS, DETAILS, DETAILS!

Finally, when you write the plan, keep in mind that others will read it, or at least part of it. They might be bankers who could lend you money, real estate professionals who want to team with you, developers who want to form relationships with you, or business partners or employees you bring on board in the future. These are just a few reasons your plan should be well crafted.

Make sure to write your business plan in complete sentences and follow a logical outline. Set off sections with short, succinct subheads. Keep it simple; don't complicate it. Make sure there are no spelling or grammar mistakes. Use a readable font, such as Times New Roman, Georgia, or my personal favorite, Arial Narrow Bold. Don't capitalize words that do not require it and do not use abbreviations if you can help it. Double-space the document and number the pages.

With your mission statement and business plan clearly written and neatly presented, you are on your way to becoming a professional Stager. This plan is not written in stone. You must be open to change and therefore should review your plan often so that you can update it as the market dictates. This is your business and your plan. It is up to you and you alone to make it work, which will mean changing it as the need arises.

Before you start to work, though, you must take into account insurance and tax consequences. The next chapter covers these important issues.

CHAPTER 4

COVER YOURSELF!

You can't sell it if you can't see it.
—BARB SCHWARZ

An important part of running a business is making sure you are covered adequately by insurance and that you have your financial records in good order. We all wish these realities were not as crucial as they are, but if you choose to ignore them or skimp on them, you do so at your own peril and expense.

I am serious when I say this. These are necessary parts of running a business, and *necessary* is the operative word. Here's the good news: Once you get your insurance policies in place with a good insurance broker whom you trust and once you set up and organize your bookkeeping strategies with a reliable CPA or tax advisor at the ready, the job is done. While you will have to be vigilant about this end of the business, you won't have to repeat these initial time-consuming processes.

THE INS AND OUTS OF INSURANCE

I say it elsewhere in this book and I will expand on it here: Before you Stage even a tiny broom closet, make sure you have business liability insurance. The right policy will cover you for any injuries sustained while you work, for anything you break, or for anything you damage.

The amount of insurance you need will vary. Talk to an insurance broker about buying a policy based on your specific requirements. The broker will help you determine how much coverage you need, but the broker will in turn need some basic information about what a Home Staging business is. Very few insurance agents know about this. They are learning about our industry, but many still do not understand it. Your job is to educate them.

Although Stagers decisively are not part of the decorating business, insurance providers categorize us as such—or at least as far as liability insurance goes. The same codes your agent uses to figure insurance for interior decorators can be used to figure yours. This should help. Insurers who understand home-based businesses such as interior design should generally be able to recommend the right insurance for a sole proprietor of a Home Staging business.

This may not be universally true. Talk to your insurance agent about coverage. He or she may have some very good ideas about how to insure your business so that you are adequately protected. I recommend that you shop around. It's probably not a good idea to accept the first estimate you hear.

I have exciting news about business liability insurance. We at StagedHomes.com have teamed with the Great American Insurance Company to offer ASP Stagers excellent coverage at low rates. Currently, the policies cost just under $550 annually, and ASP Stagers can opt to pay by the month or by the year. This is the best policy I have seen for a Home Staging business. Great American Insurance is one of North America's leading companies and I am thrilled that they get what Home Staging is all about as an industry and are willing to help us.

In general, individual policies range from about $300 to $700 a year; most Home Stagers report that they pay approximately $500. Talk to your insurance broker about the prices you will charge and the markets you expect to tackle. Ask the agent a lot of questions. Find out what is available and the amount for which you are covered in specific areas of the policy. Believe me, purchasing insurance is not too high a price to pay for peace of mind. It is always better to be safe than sorry.

I have presented here a sample yearlong Home Staging binder policy, which you can show to the broker.

SAMPLE HOME STAGING INSURANCE BINDER

This is a sample insurance binder for your reference. The fictitious insurance company is called "The Insurance Company" but all figures are based on actual policies.

Commercial Insurance Proposal Prepared for:

NAME OF YOUR STAGING COMPANY

The Insurance Company was founded in 1810 and is one of the nation's largest investment management and insurance companies, with total assets of $225.9 billion and stockholders' equity of $11.6 billion. The company is a leading provider of investment products, life insurance, and group benefits; automobile and homeowners' products; and business property-casualty insurance.

An Xpand proposal may not be bound without prior The Insurance Company underwriting approval.

**The Insurance Company
06/01/2004 to 06/01/2005**

The Insurance Company Spectrum Policy combines all of your insurance needs and packages them into one competitively priced product.

(continued)

Policy Level:

Property Coverage of Insurance	Limits
Special Property Coverage Form automatically includes the following coverages at no additional charge:	
Valuable Papers Coverage	$ 10,000
Accounts Receivable Coverage	$ 10,000
Money and Securities—Inside	$ 10,000
Money and Securities—Outside	$ 5,000
Fire Department Service Charge	$ 15,000
Fire Extinguisher Recharge	Included
Appurtenant Structures: 10% of the Building limit of insurance, but not more than $50,000 at each described premises	Included
Appurtenant Structures: 10% of the Business Personal Property limit of insurance, but not more than $5,000 at each described premises	Included
Newly Acquired or Constructed Property— Building	$ 500,000
Business Personal Property at Newly Acquired Locations	$ 250,000
Property Off-Premises—Building	$ 5,000
Property Off-Premises—Business Personal Property	$ 2,000
Automatic Increase in Building: Limit of Insurance: 4% Annual $ Included Tenant's Glass	$ 25,000
Arson Reward	$ 10,000
Definition of Premises: 1,000 feet	Included
Automatic Equipment Breakdown Coverage which includes:	Included
Mechanical Breakdown	Included
Artificially Generated Electric Current	Included

Explosion of Steam Equipment		Included
Artificially Generated Electric Current		Included
Explosion of Steam Equipment		Included
Loss or Damage to Steam Equipment		Included
Loss or Damage to Water Heating Equipment		Included

Liability Coverages	**Limits of Insurance**	**Premium**
Each Occurrence	$ 2,000,000	
General Aggregate	$ 4,000,000	Included
Products/Completed		
Operations	$ 4,000,000	Included
Personal and		
Advertising Injury	$ 2,000,000	Included
Fire Legal Liability	$ 300,000	Included
Medical Expenses	$ 10,000	Included
Hired and Nonowned		
Auto	$ 2,000,000	Included

Property Coverage	**Limits of Insurance**	**Premium**
Deductible	$ 500	
Business Income	$ 50,000	Included
Specified		

Location/Building Information:

Location No./Building No.:	001/001
Street Address:	1 Your Street
City, State and Zip Code:	Alameda, CA 94501
Protection Class : 02 Class Code:	65791
Description:	Interior Design
Construction:	Frame Year Built:
1990 Area:	450
Annual Sales/Receipts:	$75,000

(continued)

Limits of Insurance Premium	Limits of Insurance	Premium
Business Personal Property	$ 10,000	Included
Fungi Limited Coverage	$ 50,000	Included
Fungi Limited Business Interruption	30 Days	Included
Premium Summary		
	06/01/2004 to 06/01/2005	
Total Spectrum Annual Premium $533.00		

OTHER INSURANCE

In addition to business liability insurance, look into your home-owner's policy and your car insurance. Your broker might be able to revise your current homeowner's policy to cover your home-based business, but you have to ask. The policy might cover any inventory you keep in your house or garage. Review your car insurance if you use your car for business. Make sure that "in transit" items are covered. In some states, you have to adjust your automobile insurance upward if you attach a magnetic business sign to your car during business hours.

It's equally important to make sure your clients have an active homeowner's policy on their property. How do you find out? Ask! If you have any doubts, ask for a copy of their homeowner's policy and binder. If they are insured, they should have no qualms about sharing the information with you so that you can rest easy. Conversely, they need to know that you are insured and might ask for proof of your policy.

If the house is empty, there's a chance the policy has been permitted to lapse; there are other instances when policies might have lapsed as well. Under no circumstances should you stage an uninsured house—that is a poor business decision. Remember Murphy's law? Anything that can go wrong will go wrong. Don't risk letting Murphy walk through the door. Discuss the importance of a temporary policy with the homeowners before you begin Staging the house.

I do not know anyone who ever got hurt Staging a property, but there's always a first time. Require that the Stagers you bring on board or hire for a project have their own liability insurance, too. If they do not, don't hire them. This might help you decide between hiring trained professionals or hiring the kid down the street who offers to help with the heavy lifting. Work with other ASP Stagers and you will be much happier, much safer, and so much more pleased with their work, which in turn will affect your own work.

At StagedHomes.com, we train ASPs to work with other ASPs. It is exciting to have the ability to work with more than a hundred IAHSP chapters in the United States and Canada and meet fellow Stagers who have had the same training and follow the same policies and guidelines—and carry business liability insurance.

YOUR FINANCIAL LIFE

It's critical to keep a record of every transaction you make in the name of your business. This is as true for a retail store, a major airline, or a multinational corporation as it is for a small business such as yours. Why? Because this is your business, and it's good business policy to document all your transactions.

I keep records of everything. I save e-mails, drafts, and final documents, as well as other records. You never know when you might need to refer to one of them to verify information.

Understanding the income and outflow of your business funds is crucial to keeping your business afloat. For example, if you decide you need a new computer, is it in your budget? Can you afford it? Are you continuing to build inventory? Are you making your insurance premium payments? Is there anything left at the end of the month for your own needs? What if the car needs a head gasket? Or your daughter wants ballet lessons?

You get it. The list of financial demands goes on, and until you decide to take the money you earn seriously, you may find the dream of owning your own Staging business slipping away from you.

Make your business a business. Never minimize its importance to you and the world. This attitude will bring you more business, too, when you are ready for it. I wrote this book to guide you as you build your business, one step at a time. I have been doing this for more than 30 years, and with the help of this book, your business will take shape more quickly than mine did. After all, I have a lot of experience to share about the industry I developed.

BARB'S 10 RULES FOR FINANCIAL SANITY

You can make a lot of money as a successful Stager. Chapter 6 gives some solid examples of how much you can earn. You can easily make as much money or more than many real estate agents, and you don't have to worry about splitting commissions or being on the telephone at midnight negotiating a sale with a buyer or seller. But to ensure that the money you earn is money in the bank, follow these 10 sensible rules:

1. Open a checking account for your business. Use it only for the business and always for business. Do not commingle personal and business finances. This way, your business records will be separate from your personal ones. Interview bank managers to find out about the best checking account rates and programs.

2. Enter every check, and balance your checkbook monthly. If you are not comfortable doing this yourself, hire a part-time bookkeeper to help.

3. Buy enough liability insurance to protect yourself when you Stage. Upgrade your homeowner's insurance to protect your inventory and business equipment in your house or get an additional policy to cover the business as a business. As I said earlier in this chapter, talk with your insurance broker and get the policy that makes the best sense for your business.

4. Invest in a computer program such as Quicken or Quick-Books, or rely on a web site such as Ms.Money.com. Because Quicken is an easy, if not a very intense, accounting tool, you might find it convenient, as I do, to input information on Quicken and then transfer it to QuickBooks, which has more functions but is harder to learn. Hire a tutor to show you how to run these programs; you will pick them up in no time. Call the nearby community college or a local computer consulting firm to find a tech whiz you can hire privately for a few hours a week. This is not expensive, and unless you are very computer savvy, it will save you a lot of frustration.

5. Insist that anyone you hire for a project submit an invoice that includes his or her Social Security number, complete address, and the agreed-upon amount that you owe the person. Indicate directly on the invoice that it has been paid, noting both the date and the check number. If you pay by bank card, indicate this as well. File the invoices for tax records.

   Determine how many hours someone can work for you and how much you can pay them before they become an employee. Every state is different, so it's a good idea to discuss this with your accountant. My accountant told me that as long as the ASP Stagers I hired had their own businesses, I could hire them and not consider them employees, which I did not want. I ask the ASPs who work for me on projects to show me a few receipts, as proof that they have other work. Being part of the ASP network is extremely beneficial here. I can find reliable people to help me complete projects—people I can trust and people I respect.

6. Keep track of the miles you travel in your car for your business. Keep a simple mileage log in your car and record the date, travel time, and mileage. Once you get in the habit of doing this, it becomes second nature. Office supply stores even carry little books expressly for this purpose. Easy!

7. Keep track of business expenses and list them under specific categories. These are the categories I use: entertaining, office supplies, Staging supplies, Staging inventory, gas, continuing professional education, business equipment, and professional dues (such as ASP and IAHSP dues). You or your accountant may come up with other categories.

8. Keep every receipt. This means receipts for bank cards and debit cards, too. Make this a firm policy and always make sure you follow it. Once you get used to saving receipts, it is easy. Tally receipts weekly, monthly, or quarterly. This is necessary for the tax collector, but it also provides a reality check on what you spend. I have a rule for receipts: I never leave a store without writing a notation on the receipt. Believe me, it's no fun to get home after a Staging shopping spree and not be able to remember which receipts are for what, or to try to decipher receipts with faded ink or without itemized purchases. Better to be proactive and jot down a few details on the receipt when you leave the store. I take a few minutes at the checkout counter to write down what I bought and categorize the receipt (office supply, staging inventory, etc.). I move to the end of the counter so that the

next customer is not inconvenienced. When I get home, I drop the receipts into expand-a-folders labeled by category. This works for me. You may prefer another system, but it's important that you devise one that you like and will stick to.

It's also advisable to memorize the last four numbers of your credit and debit cards. Note which card you used on the receipt, too: "American Express, placemats and pillar candles, Linens-N-Things" or "Visa debit, tape, folders, and pens, OfficeMax." If there's ever a question about a bill, you will know exactly which card you used.

9. Set aside a percentage of your monthly income for inventory. This might be 2 percent, 5 percent, or 10 percent—the percentage will change as your business grows. Regardless, be consistent about doing this. You should invest in inventory where and when it makes sense by setting aside some of your earnings. If you are systematic, the money will be there when you want it. The principle is similar to that of tithing at church.

10. Pay yourself! You bring wealth to your clients, and you deserve to be paid, to be paid well, and to be paid on time. Set up a merchant account so that you can be paid via bank cards. I don't recommend that you take checks. Checks can bounce. If you send invoices, you might never get paid, or you might get paid late.

You can apply for a merchant account at your bank. This is not hard, but be prepared to answer questions and supply the bank with certain documents. Once you have a merchant account, you can ask your clients if they want to pay by bank card or debit card. This way, they have a choice—it's just not a choice to pay you by check. When you have a merchant account, you have the option to call the card number in, process it on the computer, or run it through a machine.

HOW TO OPEN A MERCHANT ACCOUNT

I worked long and hard to find a good merchant account, and once I did, I immediately switched all of my business to it. Here is how I did it, so you can do it, too.

To begin, go to www.shcmerchantaccount.com and download the merchant application, which is in PDF form. Everything is there. If you have questions, call 1-800-814-3163 to reach the ACS Merchant Application Center. Someone there will guide you through the application process.

Fax your completed application, your business license, a voided business check, and a business card or web address to 1-941-925-4448. Once you've completed this process, you should be up and running within three business days. The terms are hassle-free and there are no minimum transaction volumes or cancellation penalties with this account.

A big thanks to Bob Kenehan and Dan Skoglund for helping me find such a wonderful merchant account company that accepts credit cards without charging rates as high as the banks do. As of this writing, when you call or go to the web site to apply for your merchant account with ACS Merchant Services, they will send you, at no extra charge, my best-selling book *Home Staging: The Winning Way to Sell Your House for More Money*. How great is that?

TAXES

As Benjamin Franklin said, "In this world nothing can be said to be certain, except death and taxes."

We all have to pay taxes to the city, the state, and the federal government. When you own a business, you will have itemized deductions. My advice is to hire the best CPA or accountant you can find. Ask friends or neighbors you know who have small businesses and other professionals in your life such as your lawyer, doctor, or real estate agent for recommendations. Look for someone with expertise in handling small businesses and make sure the person is someone you like who is easy to talk to and explains things clearly.

I also recommend that your tax accountant be someone who is willing to listen to your questions and offer advice, rather than someone who is strictly a tax preparer. The difference is that the former meets with you to discuss your finances, while the latter takes your financial information and files your taxes—period.

You may find that down the road you need both a financial planner and an accountant, but if you can work with one person who does both—at least when you start out—make the most of it. Here are some questions to ask your accountant:

- What is the best way to set up my business—as a sole proprietor, as a partnership, or should I incorporate?
- When I hire assistants, should they be independent contractors or employees? (Remember how easy it is to work with other ASPs, with everyone working as independent contractors.)
- What tax forms should I file for them?
- Should I file taxes quarterly?
- How should I pay myself? How does the amount I pay myself affect my taxes?
- What is self-employment tax?
- How much of my income can I and should I reinvest in the business?
- What are the tax implications of having my office in my house?
- Can I use my car for both business and personal purposes?
- How can I deduct the wear and tear on my car?
- What questions have I overlooked?

YOUR HOME OFFICE

Chances are, you will work out of your home when you start, and you may continue to do so for years to come. The IRS is often on the alert for taxpayers who deduct home offices, so be sure to document all expenses related to the business and the office. Back up any claims with solid records. Again, consult your accountant. This is vital in the event that you get audited.

It is not a good idea to designate your dining room table as your office. Set aside a physical space, whether it's an extra bedroom, a room in the attic, or a nook off the family room. Use that area only for your Staging business. This is not where the kids do their homework or where you keep your loom or treadmill. This is a place of business that meets the IRS stipulation that it is used "regularly and exclusively" for that purpose.

The same is true of the computer. The computer you rely on for work should not be the family PC. You can deduct only hardware and software that you buy for your business—not games or study guides for the kids. Again, talk with your accountant!

When it comes to money, what matters most is what you keep, not what you earn. When you are meticulous about your records, if you budget wisely when you buy both office equipment and inventory for your Staging business, if you work with a reliable CPA and ask pertinent questions, and if you pay your taxes on time, you should be able to make a good living and do it in a smart, productive way.

TAXES AND THE INDEPENDENT CONTRACTOR

If you are sole proprietor, it makes sense to hire independent contractors when you need extra help Staging or running your office. Independent contractors are nothing more than freelancers—others who run their own small businesses. This means you do not have to file payroll taxes or pay insurance for them. It also means they are responsible for paying taxes on anything they earn while working for you.

By definition, independent contractors run their own small businesses. This means they are self-directed and work the hours they determine for themselves. And they are responsible for paying their own taxes—you do not withhold taxes from their paychecks. If the IRS decides to audit you, it does not take much for the federal government to deem that the person you pay as an independent contractor is actually your employee. One of the best ways to make sure this does not happen is to keep good records and rely on a number of different Stagers to help you complete projects. It's also crucial that you understand the laws governing freelancers in your state.

As I mentioned earlier in this chapter, whether you pay the independent contractors on an hourly or a project basis, ask them to provide you with invoices and instruct them to include their mailing address and Social Security numbers on these invoices. Mark the invoices as paid, noting the check number and date.

You will have to mail 1099 tax forms each January to everyone you have paid during the previous calendar year and file those forms with the IRS by late February. Blank 1099 forms are available in office supply stores and post offices, or you can order them directly from the IRS. You can also download them from the IRS web site at www.irs.gov/formspubs. They provide a record for the government of how much of your income you spent paying the people who help drive your business. The total amount of the 1099s is a tax deduction for you; their recipients file them with their individual 1040 forms and pay income tax on the amounts they were paid by you.

TAXES AND THE EMPLOYEE

Congratulations! Your business has grown to the point where you are able to hire salaried employees. These may be full-time or not, but you now have to file payroll taxes.

This is complicated without the help of an accountant, payroll service, or software program to calculate them, and I strongly recommend that you rely on the experts. Still, it's a good idea to have a basic understanding of what payroll taxes are. If you fail to file or if you are late with your payments, the IRS will not be happy. The penalties for either lapse are significant. You don't want to go there!

Payroll taxes include income taxes, Social Security and Medicare taxes, and unemployment taxes. You withhold income taxes from your employees' checks, you and the employee split the Social Security and Medicare payments, and you pay unemployment taxes. If your state has no income tax, you only need to withhold federal income taxes. Some states have their own rules about unemployment taxes. The safest thing to do is to hire professional advisors whom you trust and check with them every year. Rules change constantly, and it's your responsibility to keep up with them. Let the experts help.

As you can see, payroll taxes are complex. But there is more. You have to file these taxes at a local bank biweekly or monthly, depending on the size of the company. There are any number of forms to fill out, so this is where a top-notch accountant or payroll service can come to your rescue. Otherwise, you can purchase a software program, such as QuickBooks, and figure it out yourself, but I recommend that you go to the experts first. Hire a good attorney and a good CPA or accountant for your business. They will end up saving you money. You know the saying about an ounce of prevention being worth a pound of cure? It's true!

Once you have addressed the hard-core business issues covered in this chapter, you are ready to Stage houses. The next chapter covers Staging basics to get you involved in the wonderful work I so love: Home Staging. It is the joy of my life, and I hope it will be yours, as well. There is no better creative outlet than Home Staging, and nothing makes you feel happier than serving your clients by improving their lives. Home Staging is a satisfying business. As ASP Stagers like to say: "We love this business!"

CHAPTER 5

SERVICES PROVIDED BY HOME STAGERS

Let me tell you how I work.
—BARB SCHWARZ

I've told you that I created the Home Staging industry back in the early 1970s, why it's valuable to anyone who wants to sell a house, and how you can go about setting up a Home Staging business. You have written a business plan; you have consulted your accountant, lawyer, and insurance broker; and by now I am sure you are raring to go—excited to get out in the field and Stage houses!

I understand how that feels. Nothing gives me more pleasure than seeing a house lose its clutter and take on the polish that comes only with a professional Staging, preferably done by a certified ASP Stager. For me and others I know who love it, Staging is addictive as well as being a wonderful outlet for the creative genius inside every one of us. After Staging one house, you want to do more. When I Stage, I am infused with positive, refreshing energy. I can't think of anything I would rather do than Stage houses.

Best of all, the Staged house can now present itself for sale, with its best foot forward. When a property is ready for the market, it should look appealing and inviting, as though it's waiting for the next owner to fill it with laughter and joy.

STAGING BASICS

Staging is the process of transforming a home into a product that can be marketed for sale. When you Stage, you take the home out of the house by depersonalizing it. As I have said before, Staging is not about decorating, nor is it part of the design and decorating industries. Staging is part of the real estate industry. Decorating personalizes a house so that it becomes a home; Staging removes much of the personalization so that the buyers can envision moving into the space. People will not purchase a house until they can see themselves living there—something that is hard to do when the house is chockablock with the owners' collectibles, furniture, and artwork. Buyers end up being distracted by these things, rather than looking at the space itself. As I often say, you can't sell it if buyers can't see it. Whether they realize it or not, the sellers want buyers to be able to visualize how their family, their things, and their personalities will fit inside the house and imagine living there for years to come.

The work of Staging is done in steps. The first step consists of either a bid or a consultation. (Chapter 6 explains both bids and consultations.) Essentially, the difference is that when homeowners accept your bid, you do the work. When homeowners ask for a consultation, they do the work following your recommendations.

Preparing bids and consultations is a crucial part of the industry I created, which is why Chapter 6 examines them at such length. As a Stager, you will be asked to do both, and I caution you not to be concerned if you find you are doing a large number of consultations and not as many bids. In this business, consultations lead to more Staging business, as I will also explain in Chapter 6.

This chapter examines Staging basics. Chapter 9 delves more deeply into the Staging process, but here you will get the fundamentals. Keep in mind that this is not a comprehensive how-to book on Staging but a book on how to start your own business and achieve success. But to do so, you need to understand how I think Staging should be done. I have been Staging houses for 35 years, and in that time I have sold thousands of Staged properties. I have also educated well over 1 million real estate professionals about Staging and taught more than 4,200 ASP Stagers to date—and counting. (For more information on actual Staging, please read my first book, *Home Staging: The Winning Way to Sell Your House for More Money.*) What follows are some of the highlights gleaned from my many years of experience.

I teach everyone who takes one of my ASP Home Staging courses to Stage the entire property. This means from one corner of the lot to the others, as well as the inside of the house. You can't Stage a house if you don't take the time to really study it. You need perspective and distance to really *see* the property so that you can make viable recommendations to the sellers.

Although Stagers are not landscapers, it is crucial to pay attention to how a house looks from the outside, as well as how it looks on the inside. When I first arrive at a home I am going to Stage, I do not pull into the driveway. I continue past the house, glancing at it from the car window. I drive around the neighborhood and take stock of how other houses in the area present themselves. Finally, I pull over to the curb and ask myself what I see. Do bushes need trimming? Is a shingle loose? Does the house need painting? I make a similar assessment from the backyard as I walk around the property with the sellers. Trimming shrubbery, edging lawns, weeding garden beds, and removing low-hanging tree limbs are just some of the things that may need to be done to Stage the outside of a home.

Once I enter the house, I stand in the doorway of each room and take a good, hard look. What is the Staging point of the room? In other words, why does this room exist? Where is my eye drawn? If it's a bedroom, your eye should be drawn to the bed, which should always face the door. In other rooms, the eye is drawn to a large window, a pretty or dramatic view, a fireplace, or perhaps built-in bookshelves. This is the focal point, where I begin to set the Stage for that room.

I developed this Staging-eye approach when I first sold real estate back in the 1970s. In those days, I noticed that a lot of potential buyers entered a house and merely glance into each room from the doorway. They didn't even cross the threshold of the room, clearly not interested in what they saw. I recognize now that if buyers do not enter each room, they will not make an offer on the house. This was one of my earliest aha! moments. How could anyone entertain the idea of buying a particular house if the person didn't step inside every single room? I reasoned. Since then, I have relied on this doorway vantage point to guide my Staging process, and it has never let me down.

While there are numerous very specific Staging techniques (Chapter 9 examines the most critical ones), removing clutter is the most important part of Staging. People with the most clutter often have the most issues, too. This is not a hard-and-fast rule and I am no psychiatrist, but I have seen the same thing happen over and over again: Either people relinquish the clutter and their issues seem to disappear or they work on their issues and then they are ready to Stage. My keen observation after Staging thousands and thousands of homes is that when a Stager removes the clutter from the house, the homeowners relax and let go of any resistance they might have to selling the property. This is why I say that Staging brings peace to the property.

What could be better than that? We all want peace and we all want prosperity. Staging accomplishes both.

Beyond removing clutter, Staging involves cleaning the house from top to bottom. By this, I mean that the place should be what I call "Q-tip clean." Your role as a Stager is not to clean the house. Aren't you happy about that? It is customary—and one of the policies I recommend that all ASP Stagers employ—to ask the sellers to have the house professionally cleaned before it is Staged. This extends to professional window washing, professional carpet cleaning, and professional painting.

When professionals clean the house for Staging it entails wiping scuff marks from the walls and doing their best to rid the carpets of stains and grime, as well as performing a thorough general cleaning, inside and out. (The carpets will probably need professional cleaning. It is rare to see a home where they do not.)

Cleaning also means getting rid of any odors that might turn off potential buyers. No homeowners want to hear that their house smells like their beloved kitty, but cats seem to be the number one culprits when it comes to odors. Dogs, too, are a challenge, as are cigarette or cigar smoke and heavy cooking smells. Sometimes getting rid of odors is as easy as removing certain rugs, drapes, and furniture. Sometimes it demands more stringent measures, such as wiping down the walls with a solution of bleach and water. I also recommend—and use—an amazing product developed by a scientist in my hometown of Seattle, Washington, that works wonders with persistent odors. Called PureAyre, it is made from plant enzymes and is sold on my company's web site, StagedHomes.com. Professional Stagers love it, and unlike some of the other products available today, it requires no scary warning labels. This product is safe to use around babies, pets, and food.

Once the homeowners have lived up to their commitment to take care of whatever you and they have discussed in terms of your professional policies, such as cleaning, painting, or landscaping, you can Stage the property.

Your Staging could involve packing up collectibles, knick-knacks, books, and photographs in an effort to streamline the look of the house. It could entail removing furniture from overfilled rooms, replacing a piece in the living room with another from a bed-room to create a welcoming vignette, or perhaps getting rid of heavy drapes, replacing them with a light, airy valance fashioned from a pretty bedsheet. It could mean rehanging artwork so that it makes a bold yet pleasing statement on a large wall or setting a dining table with an attractive cloth, colorful chargers, and bright white plates. (Please, never set tables with cutlery or leave a knife block filled with knives on the kitchen counter. This is a safety issue for the real estate agent, who may be alone in the house with strangers.)

Staging a bedroom might mean angling a bed in a small room to create the illusion of spaciousness; Staging a small bathroom could mean rolling towels and tying them with raffia. You might fill a flowerpot with inexpensive but colorful impatiens or gerani-ums to bring splashes of color to the front steps. These and other Staging techniques shape up houses in a way that home buyers appreciate and respond to.

If the outside of the house looks shabby or nearly every room is painted an overpowering hue and the homeowners need to remedy the situation, this can represent a substantial financial outlay for them. This is one of those times when it pays you to use the word *investment,* because this is precisely what it is: an investment in the final outcome.

Paint is one of the most inexpensive ways to spruce up a house, but the labor can add up. Because the homeowners are selling the house, the paint job needs to be neat and attractive, but there is no need to use superexpensive products. Good paint often is on sale at places like Wal-Mart and Home Depot, and even at the Habitat for Humanity stores. Replacing a kitchen floor or painting the exterior of the home is pricier than painting a room. You and the homeown-ers will have to decide where to make the needed investments in the house, but if you remind them that Staging will cost them less than the first reduction of the sale price of the home, I suspect they will opt for the suggested fix-ups.

I can't sufficiently stress to ASP Stagers that Staging is not about *spending* money but, instead, about *making* money for the clients. If you, as a professionally trained ASP Stager, believe the clients need to make a relatively sizable investment to sell the house, then it's your responsibility to work with the homeowners and help them understand that this investment will pay off big-time.

People respond more readily to the concept of investing than to that of spending. I teach sellers that when they Stage their properties to sell, they are investing in them. If they conceive of the necessary expenditures as extra spending rather than an investment, they will be resistant. If they view these expenses as a valuable investment, they will be ready to put their money on the table, knowing they will make it back, and then some. See Table 5.1.

Table 5.1   Your Return on Home Improvement Investments

Improvement	Typical Cost	Increase in Sales Price	Average Return	Agents Who Recommend
Lighten and brighten	$86–$110	$768–$935	769%	84%
Clean and declutter	$305–$339	$2093–$2378	594%	91%
Fix plumbing and electrical	$338–$381	$922–$1,208	196%	63%
Landscape and trim	$432–$506	$1,594–$1,839	266%	72%
Staging	**$212–$1,089**	**$2,275–$2,841**	**169%**	76%
Kitchen and bath upgrades	$1,546–$2,120	$3,823–$4,885	138%	83%
Repair flooring	$1,531–$1,714	$2,267–$1,714	50%	62%
Paint exterior walls	$2,188–$2,381	$2,907–$3,233	34%	57%
Replace carpeting	$2,602–$2,765	$3,585–$3,900	39%	65%

THE SELLERS' CONCERNS

Home Staging is all about educating the homeowners first and then working with the house to set the scene. Once sellers grasp what Staging is and why and how it's done, they are ready to get on board. But remember: If they are reluctant, they are not thinking of their home as a product and they may not be ready to sell. This is why it's so important to interview the sellers as well as the real estate agent. As I have found in the more than 30 years I have been Staging houses, sellers resist Staging for two reasons:

1. They really do not want to sell. The reason for this could be as simple as they don't want the inconvenience of having the public traipse through their house—although if this is so, there probably are other, deeper reasons in play.
2. They were poorly educated about the benefits and realities of Staging by someone other than you. This might have been a neighbor who suggested the neighborhood was not high-end enough to justify Staging, or it might have been an uninformed colleague who casually said she had heard Staging was very expensive and could cost as much as $90,000. Of course, neither reason is sound. In truth, Staging sells houses in every market, high and low, and Staging should never cost a lot of money. Any homeowner who spends tens of thousands of dollars to Stage a house has been taken advantage of big-time!

I work in steps and never jump ahead of myself—and I mean *never*. I do not go to the next step until I am finished with the step before it. I believe in systems, and Staging is a system. It is all about organized, purposeful presentation. The steps move sellers forward methodically so that they are best served as they prepare the house for sale. This deliberate pace builds trust, relaxes jittery sellers, and shows the more demanding sellers that you are dedicated to being professional.

Working in steps says: "I value your home and your business. I want to work with sellers who are interested in working with me, and who want it done right." This puts you in a leadership role and positions you to educate the sellers. If you don't lead, the homeowners will want to take charge, and that can be disastrous. You are the pro, and you know how to make the Staging work most effectively. Explaining to the potential clients how you work up front ensures that your relationship with them will be good throughout the entire project—and they will recommend you to their friends.

Working in steps helps you establish your credibility and build a foundation for a good working relationship. Your attitude is important, too. People will pick up on your commitment, your intent, and how much you believe in what you are doing. You are the professional, you have the knowledge, training, and ideas. "And if you aren't sold, you can't sell!" I always say.

You should convey that you respect the homeowners' concerns and their valuable piece of real estate. Working through the process step-by-step demonstrates this; it shows that you are dedicated to the process as a Home Staging professional. If you learn anything from this book, I hope it is this: Work in steps. It's the only way to go!

STEPS FOR WORKING WITH THE SELLERS

I begin by walking through the house, taking pictures, and complimenting the homeowners on the property. This is easy to do. Mention those things about the property and the contents of the house that appeal to you. There is no reason to be phony about this. Anyone who likes houses as much as Stagers do—and I am the number one believer of this—can always find something to like.

To build the sellers' confidence and demonstrate that I have successfully Staged other houses, I leave my credentials and illustrative examples of Staged properties for the sellers to look at in my Career Book. This is a carefully constructed loose-leaf binder (I will discuss it in more detail later). When I return the next day for a second meeting, the sellers have looked through my Career Book and are usually more than ready to discuss Staging in detail. The proof of my commitment to the profession is in the credentials and the Career Book. Both show that I know how to Stage homes, and the letters of reference reassure homeowners that I have been successful and reliable.

My message to sellers is that Staging is not about spending their money but about making an investment in their property that they will get back many times over. When I explain that the up-front investment in Staging their home amounts to less than a reduction on the sale price of the home once it's on the market, sellers get it. This is one of the most convincing arguments for them. They quickly grasp the principle of making the small investment in Staging to bring the much larger return. This return is top dollar for the property, regardless of the local real estate market. Staging is a way to build equity in your home. One of my associates, Dan Skoglund, ASP, came up with a concept we call ROSI, or Return on Staging Investment. (You may have heard about ROI, but insert the "S" and the term is even more powerful!)

Chapter 6 will explain how to set fees to ensure that you are well and fairly paid and that the homeowners are never asked to make an unreasonable investment. I tell homeowners that if any Stager advises that they spend vast amounts of money, they should run the other way. Look for another Stager, preferably one who is a certified Accredited Staging Professional (ASP). These people are trained in how to Stage homes creatively without spending a lot of money. At StagedHomes.com, our philosophy is that ASP Stagers should be paid for their creativity and not for spending money needlessly.

As I explained earlier, Staging is not about the condition of the house. The real estate agent is the person to discuss the house's condition with the homeowners—problems such as a leaky roof, rotted window frames, or a moldy basement. These sorts of issues have a lot to do with how the house is priced for sale. The Stager's job is to Stage the house once it is just about ready to go on the market, so that the real estate agent can market it as a Staged property and get it sold in short order.

I teach my students to be honest and open about the Staging process and to include the homeowners as part of the Staging team, then hold them accountable for getting their part done. The homeowners' role in Staging could be as simple as removing their valuables and packing up the china, or as involved as painting a room. I urge Stagers to be sensitive to the homeowners' feelings. No one wants to hear that his or her house is dirty or smells like cats, but we owe it to our clients to notify them of anything that could prevent the house from selling. In doing so, we help them understand that we want to work with them to Stage the house so that it sells in a reasonable amount of time and for top dollar. Adhering to the step-by-step approach helps you be successful. Staging is a process, and your clients understand this when you work in steps.

I always tell my clients what I intend to do and when I will do it. I also inform them when I have completed a task. I keep lines of communication open throughout the entire process. In the many thousands of Stagings I have done, I have had only one client turn to me in anger when she entered her Staged home. Bracing myself to hear just about anything, I asked her why. "Because I didn't think of doing this myself!" she responded.

THE VALUE OF STAGING

Staging works! It is a creative process that delivers a big punch and tangible results. When the house sells quickly, and for the asking price or more, the sellers are spared the emotional trauma of a long, drawn-out process. Staging facilitates the next step in the family's life. Because of this, I like to say that ours is a "happy business."

Staging benefits many people other than the sellers. Appraisers like to appraise Staged homes, loan officers like to hear that a house is being Staged because they know this means they will be doing business very soon with the sellers and/or the buyers, real estate agents like Staged homes because they sell quickly and for good prices in any market, and neighbors love that the house is being Staged because it will sell quickly, which means they soon will welcome a new resident and their own property values will hold steady or increase.

Staging has changed the real estate market. Both industries— Staging and real estate—will continue to evolve in the coming years. When the market is good, Staging brings in top dollar, which often means an amount over the asking price; when the market is slow, Staging keeps it moving.

ASP Stager Diane Burdette sent me an e-mail not too long ago. "Dear Barb," she wrote, "I just wanted you to know that after Staging my own home, I had a garage sale and decided to put a For Sale By Owner sign in the yard. I actually sold my home at the garage sale, to the first people who looked at it! It sold for more money per square foot than any home in the area. Staging definitely works," she concluded.

Diane explained that she had put her house on the market for several months the year before and had received only a single low-ball offer. She took the house off the market and signed up for my three-day ASP Staging course.

She Staged the property and, with the advice of other professionals, priced her house high, but not unreasonably so. "I knew I had to present it perfectly," she said. "I had to 'wow' buyers." When she put the For Sale By Owner sign in the front lawn during the garage sale, she thought it would be a good way to test the waters. We know how that turned out. Not a bad return for a garage sale and a Staged home!

I hear stories like Diane's all the time. Each one strengthens my resolve to spread the word about Staging and fills me with indescribable joy.

Increasing numbers of sellers are beginning to understand that Staging can increase the sale price of their house. I have found that a carefully Staged house can sell for 6 to 20 percent more than the list price in a modest neighborhood. In a high-end neighborhood, this can be as much as 20 to 25 percent more. Staging creates a ripple effect: It impacts the homeowners, the real estate agent, the neighborhood, and the mortgage company. This in turn affects the economy in general.

I have seen, too, how Staging affects the sale of new construction. Stagers may be asked to Stage the model homes for a development or a few of the houses that have not sold and still stand empty. But it goes even further.

StagedHomes.com was contacted by Remington Homes, one of the largest builders in the Chicago area. The company is offering prospective buyers $1,500 to have an ASP Stager Stage their current house. The professionals at Remington Homes recognize that the ASP Staged house will sell rapidly and for good money, and the delighted homeowners will then be able to purchase a new house in one of Remington's developments. What an ingenious idea! It's a winner for everyone.

I am proud to see builders such as Remington Homes and Pulte Homes realize that prospective buyers most likely need to sell a property before they can buy one of the builders' houses. It's smart business for the builders to promote Home Staging. Years ago, when I was first Staging houses in the Seattle area, a good number of my referrals were from builders. I saw then what a brilliant idea it was to team up with builders. I see now that it's an idea whose time has come. When builders as sophisticated as Remington Homes and Pulte Homes show such faith in Home Staging, it's easy to see that it is a viable business with a serious purpose.

Best of all, Staging is an industry that is just beginning to come into its own. We are riding a wave of interest and are looking at an extensive period of long-term growth. Happily, my years of hard work have resulted in a strong foundation on which the industry can build. For this I am forever grateful. It has been a true gift to me to be able to change the lives of sellers, buyers, real estate agents, and all the wonderful people involved in the Home Staging business.

The good news is that the field is wide open. Increasing numbers of people will benefit from the power of Home Staging in coming years!

CHAPTER 6

BIDS, FEES, AND CONSULTATIONS

Longevity on the market means one thing: reduction in price.
—BARB SCHWARZ

The heart of any Staging business consists of three professional services that you can provide: consultations, bids, and the actual Staging work. This chapter addresses the first two; Chapters 5 and 9 address the actual Staging work.

WHAT IS A CONSULTATION?

Chances are very good that a consultation will begin with a telephone call or e-mail from a real estate agent. "Can you consult with my clients about Staging their home? They will do the work," the agent might say. "They need you to tell them what to do." If a seller calls you directly, the request will be similar. As a result of all

I have done to spread the word about Home Staging through the media, more and more sellers are contacting Stagers directly.

During a Home Staging consultation, you, the Stager, walk through the house and around the grounds with the homeowners. After this quick tour, you take time to prepare your report and set your fee. Explain to the homeowners that you will view the rooms again and spend some time in the yard, by yourself. Explain that you will take notes and use your digital camera, and when you finish your detailed walk-through, you will need a quiet place to prepare the preliminary report and figure the fee.

I learned the hard way how important it is to let your creativity flow while in the house, without the distraction of the homeowners or real estate agent. They can be on the premises, of course, but not by your side as you do your work. Some homeowners will be tempted to follow you around the house and ask lots of questions. Politely but firmly explain that you need to concentrate on the job at hand and that you will happily answer any and all questions once the homeowners have reviewed your consultation report and paid your fee.

While you are there, prepare a preliminary handwritten Home Staging report and your fee. If the sellers say they want to start work right away based on the preliminary report, insist on your fee before you leave. Either way, go back to your office and type the formal consultation report. The next day, hand the report to the homeowners in a businesslike folder or binder. More detail about how to do this appears later in this chapter, but essentially you should include photographs and a cover letter. Always make three copies of the consultation report—one for the homeowners, one for the real estate agent, and one for your files. The report should outline what you advise the sellers to do to attract buyers.

I explain to the homeowners that I expect payment before I hand over the formalized report. Once I have payment, I sit down with them and go over my suggestions and answer any questions.

Currently, most referrals for consultations and bids come from the real estate community, but more and more are coming directly from homeowners. Just as sellers call an agent when they want to list their house, they may also contact a Stager. I predicted this would happen a number of years ago—and I was right.

Regardless of who makes the initial contact, you must be prepared to educate both the agent and the sellers about Staging. People trust Stagers who take time to teach them about the craft. I feel strongly about this, and it's why I came up with the phrase "Let me tell you how I work," which I use to preface any consultation.

When you get the call from the real estate agent, ask him or her about the house. Ascertain whether it's on the market or will be soon. It is equally important to talk with the sellers on the telephone before you visit the house; ask them the same questions you asked the agent. The differences between their answers might surprise you. For instance, the homeowners may have a very different idea of how urgent it is to sell the house, or they may believe the agent has not done enough to market the house. The more you know, the better prepared you will be for the consultation. Questions to ask both the agent and the homeowners should include the following:

- What is the square footage of the property? This is important to give you an idea of the scope of work and time you will need to complete (and price) your consultation.
- How much clutter is in the house? Are there rooms that are empty? Where do the homeowners store their extra things?
- If the house is not already on the market, what is the target market date?
- Is the house a brand-new listing?
- If not a new listing, how long has the house been on the market?
- Ask the agent why he or she thinks the house has not sold yet. Ask the sellers the same question.
- What, if any, price reductions have there been? Knowing that the agent has already dropped the price lets you reassure the

sellers, as well as the agent, that an investment in Staging the home (or listing) is less than a price reduction on the home (or listing). This is one of the great truths of Home Staging.

- How motivated are the sellers? Sellers who want to move are always more eager and receptive to Staging their property with you.

- What is the basic floor plan of the house? Knowing something about the floor plan will give you a heads-up before you visit the house. By discussing the floor plan with the real estate agent and/or the sellers, you may learn of a problem that requires some creative Staging—and if you have the chance to think about it before you see the house, you will be able to impress the homeowners with a useful, innovative idea. Have either the agent or the sellers walk you through the floor plan on the phone. This tactic works. For example, ask them what you see when you come in the front door. Is the living room straight ahead, the dining room to the right, and the kitchen beyond that? You get the idea.

- Ask the agent what the list price is. I do not ask homeowners about price during the phone call. This is because I do not want them to get the impression I base my fee on the price of the house. If they ask, tell them truthfully that your fee is determined by the amount of clutter and the size of the house. No matter what anyone says, no one can estimate the amount of clutter if they live in the house. You have to walk through the house to gauge it!

- Ask the sellers what they know about Staging. Do not be surprised if they ask you the same question. They are looking for your bona fides, and who can blame them? This is where having your ASP designation helps significantly. You can point to it as a guarantee that you are well trained and reassure the sellers that I have built a national reputation around the ASP designation and certification.

- Ask the homeowners in what way they believe Staging will

help them sell their house. It's important that you know how much the real estate agent has told them to give you an idea of how much educating you will have to do yourself.

When you talk to the homeowners directly, you can educate them properly and control your communication and relationship with them. Some agents will try to maintain control and be the go-to person between you and the seller. I recommend that you not allow this to happen. Make it part of your professional policy that you talk and deal directly with the homeowners. Point out that the property belongs to them and that it is therefore crucial that you speak personally to them—not through the real estate agent.

WHAT TO CHARGE FOR A CONSULTATION

Understandably, the homeowners will ask you what you charge. This is often their first question. While you must explain that you can't determine the exact fee until you see the house, you can give them a range or state that the price is usually below $500. Tell them that it depends on the size of the house, the floor plan, and the amount of Staging that needs to be done. Assure them that these details will be included in the written report. I usually charge between $350 and $500, but I have charged as little as $250 and as much as $1,000 or more for a consultation.

Some Stagers choose to charge on the basis of square footage only. If you decide this works for you, you can state your fees to the homeowners over the telephone. For example, for 1,000 to 2,000 square feet you might charge $250; for 2,000 to 3,000 square feet, $350; and for 3,000 to 4,000 square feet, $500, and so on up the line. This is a fair and easy way to price. Since the average consultation takes two to three hours of your time, plus travel, you owe it to yourself and your clients to expect fair compensation for your time, effort, and expertise. Here's another way to look at this: How much is it worth to you to give up a half day of your life? When you begin your career as a Home Stager, you may be tempted to give your time away to gain clients and experience, but at some point you will decide that you need to be paid.

Every spring, at the annual ASP Home Staging Convention, I take a survey of consultation fees. In 2006, the average price was $375 for a consultation that took two and a half hours. This figure is based on prices in major metropolitan areas such as Houston, Kansas City, and San Francisco. When you break that number down to a rate of $150 an hour, the pay is good.

Setting your fee is a process of trial and error, from which you will learn as you go. Before you learned to drive, you read the driving manual and sat behind the wheel of a car, but you did not really know how to drive until you actually felt the road under the wheels in a moving vehicle. This is true of setting consultation fees, too. You might set a few too low or too high in the beginning, but soon you will have a very good idea of what to charge. Each house and every seller is different. If you work in steps and explain the process to the client as you go, you will be successful.

I believe that in the future we will see our fees rise as our work as ASP Stagers is recognized as a critical factor—if not *the* critical factor—in the sale of a home.

THE CONSULTATION REPORT

Write the consultation report by listing every room and outside area and detailing exactly what needs to be done to Stage it. Bear in mind that the sellers are going to do this work themselves, so be prepared to make compromises. Few sellers understand what ASP Stagers learn during their training course, nor do they have the know-how, energy, inclination, or time to Stage their house as thoroughly or creatively as a trained Home Stager does. Nevertheless, with your help and a thorough consultation report, their house will be Staged. It may not be as creatively turned out as it would be if professionally Staged, but it will be picked up, packed up, and cleaned up, and have the right amount of furniture and accessories in every room, as instructed by you.

I summarize and prioritize the consultation report by ending with a must-do list with only a few tasks. When you go through the consultation with the clients, you will see that most did not expect to have to take on this much work. If they seem worried, refer them to the must-do list to put their minds at rest. These are the most important things they need to do.

This list might include suggestions such as these:

- Remove all clutter from kitchen counters and bathroom counters. Store small appliances and items underneath the sink or in cupboards and out of sight.
- Replace the upstairs bathroom shower curtain with a solid white one, and remove the bathroom rug and toilet seat cover. Move the rug from the kitchen to the bathroom and put it in front of the sink because the colors of the rug work better in the bath.
- Clean all light switch plates, all doorknobs, all carpeted rooms, all vinyl floors, and all windows throughout the house.
- Pack up one-third of the books on the bookshelves in the den and the office and put them away to make the book-shelves look less cluttered.
- Trim the bushes in front of the house to below the windows, which will let the light into the rooms. Round them from the top with clippers and remove all dead branches and leaves. Pull dead plants from the kitchen window box and replant with thriving, colorful flowers.

You get the idea.

Type and double-space the report and then make three copies, one for the homeowners, one for the real estate agent, and one for your files. Attach appropriate photos to illustrate your points and suggestions. For example, a photo of the overgrown plants crowding the windows in the front of the house might make the sellers sit up and take notice. The report provides a fresh pair of eyes through which the homeowners can see what needs to be done. As we all know, it's hard to really see things when you live with them everyday. Homeowners need our help, as Stagers, to evaluate their houses and properties.

Make sure you present the report in person if at all possible. This way, you can go over your suggestions and answer any questions. Sit at a table with the homeowners and review the consultation page by page. By now, the homeowners should have looked at your Career Book and, if you are an ASP Stager, watched the DVDs *How to Stage Your Home to Sell for Top Dollar!* and *How to Price Your Home to Sell for Top Dollar!*

Take this opportunity to plant the seeds of Staging the house for the homeowners. To make sure that the home is properly Staged, offer to come back once they have completed what you suggest. This way, you can fine-tune the Staging, if need be. Explain that this means you will "certify" the house as being Staged. Let them know how much you will charge by the hour for fine-tuning their work. Many ASP Stagers include the fine-tuning fee in their original consultation fee, charging for it up front. This helps ensure that your recommendations are carried out and the house is truly Staged.

It is very important that upon the presentation of your consultation you make the homeowners aware that you are available to do as little or as much as they want. Some sellers will be comfortable performing the work outlined in your report, but others will be overwhelmed by the scope of what you are suggesting and will want and need help. This is the perfect opportunity to make yourself available to do some actual Staging work for them. Sellers can get tired Staging their houses. They may do a few bedrooms and then decide to call you in to Stage the rest of the house. This does not happen all the time, but it happens more often than you might think.

Furthermore, when you tell the homeowners, "I can do as little or as much as you like," you open the door to Staging. Believe it or not, if you do not offer this, the homeowners might not think of it themselves. As I often say, "People don't know what you don't tell them!" Make it clear to the sellers that you will happily give them a bid for Staging, should they decide that is what they want. When homeowners voice interest in turning the consultation into a bid, some Stagers sweeten the pot by offering to fold the consultation fee into the Staging fee. I don't recommend this; I think you should get paid separately for the work you have already done. A doctor doesn't credit your blood test fees to your X-ray fees. Each service is independent of the other, and Stagers deserve to be paid for every service they provide.

Present the homeowners with an invoice and, as you explained on the telephone and now in person, collect your payment before you leave. This is why I recommend that you open a merchant account so that you can accept credit and debit cards (see Chapter 4 for information on how to open a merchant account with low fees). Doing so will make you seem more professional and also make it easier to collect. You want to get paid, right? Right!

Consultations are usually paid for by the homeowners, but many real estate agents set themselves apart from other agents by hiring an ASP Stager and providing a Staging consultation as a part of their marketing services. Agents appreciate having a third-party expert educate sellers about Staging so that they don't have to. (I have met very few agents who like to discuss the odor of the kitty litter or the mildewed basement carpet with clients; Stagers are trained to do this.)

Real estate agents who take one of my ASP Home Staging courses are usually astonished by the fabulous work our Stagers-in-training do during the class. Once they complete the course and get their ASP real estate agent designation, they freely tout the benefits of hiring ASP Stagers to Stage properties. I am proud to say that many of these agents now include the services of an ASP Stager in their marketing plan. We create wealth for home sellers and thus for real estate agents, too.

THE BID PROPOSAL

As with a consultation, a bid usually starts with a call from a real estate agent. However, an increasing number are being initiated with a call from the sellers. Just as with the consultation, you should first interview the party who calls you, and then the other party (whether that is the agent or the homeowners), too. See the questions that start on page 77 for what to ask during this interview. Whether for a bid or for a consultation, the questions are the same.

There is no charge for a bid proposal, and an accepted bid leads directly to a Staging project. There is always a charge for a consultation, which may or may not lead to a bid and then to a Staging. When you begin with the bid, you are going for a full Staging for an occupied or vacant property.

To prepare a bid, you must walk through the house and around the grounds just as you would for a consultation. As you go, take lots of pictures—even more than for a consultation. You will pore over these photos in the privacy of your own office as you decide how to Stage the rooms. If you work with a team, you can share the photos with your teammates.

Just as with a consultation, ask to meet with the homeowners. When you do, leave them your Career Book and, if you are an ASP Stager, my DVD, *How to Price Your Home to Sell for Top Dollar!* When the bid is accepted, give them the *How to Stage Your Home to Sell for Top Dollar!* DVD to watch.

Tour the house with the homeowners and as you proceed, begin to Stage the house in your head. Jot down notes as ideas occur to you; you don't need to share them with the homeowners.

The homeowners might ask you some very direct questions: "Do you think the color of this bedroom is too much?" "What about the overstuffed chair in my daughter's room? Should it go?" "Do you think we have too much glassware in the corner cupboard?" You might answer a couple of simple questions to demonstrate your expertise and be conversational—and because you never want to be rude—but this is a good time to say, "If you want me to make specific recommendations, then I will happily give you a consultation now or later, and there is a charge for that. I want to make sure that I am here for the service you really want. Would you rather that I perform a Home Staging consultation or continue with the bid and Staging proposal?"

When the sellers ask too many questions, this response immediately makes them aware that I am not there to answer questions at that time. Politely but firmly, I explain that if I were to answer a lot of questions during the bid process, I would have to charge them for a consultation. Once you start making bids, you will agree with this approach. Your knowledge is valuable and you cannot give it away for nothing, nor can you squander your time answering questions that should wait until you have written up the bid. Normally, when sellers hear this, they step back and wait for the process to play out. All you are doing is educating them about the process in a professional manner. This is a way to take control of the meeting and make sure the clients know the difference between a bid and a consultation. I find that the sellers (or the real estate agent, if present) usually say something like, "Oh, no, please continue with your work for the bid. We can ask the questions the next time we get together."

When I make these points during my ASP Staging courses, students have responded gratefully: "I have been giving sellers too much of my time when I visit the house to give them a bid and then I don't get hired." If you provide too many ideas and opinions up front, the sellers may not feel any need to hire you, and that's not why you are there.

I recommend that you take half an hour or less to go through the house, talk with the sellers and/or real estate agent, and make notes on what you see. Go back to your office and prepare the bid. This is when you put in a lot of time.

Following is a sample bid.

Sample Bid

(Your Logo/Letterhead)

Seller Name	Agent Name
Property Address	Target Market Date

Staging Fee	$ 2,500
(Includes Staging time, list of rooms to be Staged, complimentary travel time, load and unload, de-Staging and number of assistants)	
Your Accessory/Furniture Rental	$ 500
TOTAL (due upon completion)	$ 3,000
Furniture Company Rental	$ 1,100
(To be rented from Furniture Company. Researched and listed separately)	

I am here to meet your time and budget requirements.
Should you have any questions, please let me know.
I look forward to working with you.

_____

Signature

PREPARING THE BID

Keep the financial part of the bid to a single page. Type and space it neatly and clearly. Include your name and contact information at the top, with your logo if you have one. Include the sellers' names and address on one side at the top of the page and then the name and address of the agent on the other top side of the page. The bid should have the target date when the house will go on the market, and then it should explain the Staging fee.

Other parts of the bid should list what the Staging will entail:

- Number of rooms to be Staged (be specific and name each room).
- Outdoor areas to be Staged (name each area).
- The creative Staging time fee, which covers innovative ideas as well as the physical Staging. Set the fee by the project, not by the hour. If you say something will take four or six hours, the seller may balk and insist you are taking too much time. For this reason, make it a flat fee. Let's say the Staging fee is $3,200. Clearly explain that this includes Staging as well as paying the five Stagers whom you plan to hire to help. This way, the sellers see the work as a project, which is how you want them to see it.
- Travel time (many Stagers make this complimentary).
- Loading and unloading time.
- De-Staging time (removing things when the house sale closes).
- Number of assistants (if applicable).
- Rental of accessories or furniture that you have in your inventory.
- Furniture from a rental company (most often necessary for vacant houses; I add this to the bottom, below my own bid, as an extra service). Chapter 9 discusses renting furniture at

greater length, but if rentals are required, I strongly recommend that you never act as the financial go-between for the sellers and the furniture rental company. The sellers should pay the company directly. You can recommend a company and even offer to pick out the pieces, but never front the money.

A sample bid might consist of your fee ($2,500), accessory rentals ($500), and furniture rental ($1,100). The bottom line for the homeowners is $4,100.

In the broad scheme of things, this is a small investment and amounts to a lot less than reducing the property's price by $10,000 or $15,000, or more. The average price reduction on homes in the United States and Canada is 5 to 10 percent of the asking price, which is a lot of money. With those percentages, a house that lists for $500,000 will drop by $25,000 to $50,000. It's easy to see that $4,100 is a preferable investment.

There are many ways to Stage your bid and make it look professional. I recommend that most bids be approximately 10 pages. Here are some things you can add to dress it up:

- A fancy binder with your logo or theme on the binder.
- An attractive cover page.
- A thank-you letter to the sellers for the opportunity to make the bid.
- Before-and-after photos of several rooms that you have Staged for previous clients.
- A few testimonials from satisfied former clients.
- Photos of this house.
- The bid page.
- Statistics supporting that Staged homes sell more quickly and for more money than others.
- Your mission statement or code of ethics.

Just as I do with a consultation report, I make three copies of the bid: one for the homeowners, one for the real estate agent, and one for me. When I bind the bid I include a cover letter that says I am pleased to be presenting the bid and I assure the sellers that they can contact me with questions. I attach photos of the rooms and outdoor areas to be Staged. At the bottom of the financial page, which should be the first page of the bid, I usually add a note that says: "I really look forward to working with you. I am here to work within your budget and time constraints to Stage your home to help it sell for top dollar."

Finally, I enclose a handwritten note with the bid. It usually says something like "I love your home! Thank you for the opportunity to work with you and to present this bid." This short, handwritten message means a lot to most sellers, and it helps you stand out. It shows your sincerity, which of course needs to be authentic, and says that you go the extra mile for your clients.

THE OTHER SIDE OF THE BID

Just as consultations can lead to bids and Staging work, bids can lead to consultations. Homeowners might be overwhelmed by the price and on the verge of turning you down. Do not let this happen.

When you present the bid, tell the homeowners how you work. Say, "I can do as little or as much as you want," which is a powerful promise that lets the homeowners know that if the figure is too high, there are other options.

An option might be to customize the Staging by not doing quite as much in designated parts of the house. The house will still be Staged, but the less important rooms, such as guest rooms and attics, will not be as intricately Staged. Another option could be to offer to consult on the house. You've already done most of the work, so now you need to set a fee and prepare the consultation report. The homeowners might happily take you up on this—only to turn around several weeks later and ask you to come back and Stage the house!

SETTING YOUR FEES

We all love to Stage homes. If you did not, you probably would not be reading this book. Many of us might even say, "I love Staging so much that I would do it for free!" Doing it for free is not an option for my readers. Home Staging is a career that requires planning and creativity at the highest level. It necessitates budgeting and smart shopping. And, most important, you must love to work closely with people and approach the job with a service-minded attitude.

As much as we all enjoy Staging for the creative outlet it provides, make no mistake about the fact that we are running businesses. Part of doing so is making money, which is imperative if we want to continue doing the work we love.

I am here to help. My 35 years of experience should make it relatively easy for you to jump into the wonderful world of Home Staging with both feet and start running toward your goal of building a successful business.

Also in your favor is the fact that Staging is one of the fastest-growing careers for small business owners in the world. It attracts people from all walks of life and past experiences and is a profession that can be organized to fit your schedule.

Being successful in any venture requires smart business sense and firm dedication. A good business plan, as discussed in Chapter 3, will help you understand how to make money and can keep you on track. Beyond that, you must have a good idea of how much money you need to earn to keep the business viable. As your Home Staging business grows, so will your revenue stream, but first you have to get started.

When I give ASP Staging courses and teach students how to

start their own Staging businesses, I urge them to be professional at all times—and this means not being hesitant to discuss money. Sure, none of us can wait to roll up our sleeves, get into a house, and make it shine with our brilliant Staging techniques, but unless we get paid fairly for our efforts, we are not running a business. We are playing at Staging as a hobby.

To get paid equitably, you have to believe in your own worth. This does not mean picking a figure out of thin air and saying, "Okay, I want to earn $150 an hour." It means understanding the real estate market in general and your Staging market specifically.

Many Stagers charge by the hour, or at least set their fees based on an hourly rate, whether the client is told what that rate is or not. You should, instead, consider charging by the project. What is this project worth? How much work and creativity will it take? Is this project worth $500? Is it worth $1,000? More?

When you prepare a bid or consultation, you will likely figure the number of ASP Stagers you need to hire to work with you on the basis of both your hourly rate and the extra work required. So you must calculate what you need to complete the project and then add to that figure the expense of hiring other Stagers. For example, if the project is a $1,000 job for you and you plan to hire two Stagers at $400 each, the bid is $1,800—and this is before you add any rentals. When you become an ASP Stager, you can often hire new graduates to work just for the experience. It's one of the benefits of getting your ASP certification and networking with others. I don't suggest hiring non-ASP Stagers when you are an ASP. You never know how well trained they are, whether they have insurance, and how well they will work with the rest of the team.

When you add up the rates and charges, you can present the clients with a flat fee. As I have already said, homeowners want to know the bottom-line dollar figure. Showing them how you charge by the hour for a bid complicates matters. It is much better to say to your clients, "I will Stage your home professionally and complete all that I have outlined in the bid for $X." And then stick to this figure.

There is much more to pricing than just figuring the Staging time. You must consider all the factors that are part of the project before you begin, once you are working, and after you are finished Staging. For instance, you might walk through a house that needs Staging and decide it will take you six hours to do it. Add to that the hours you spend with the client, the time you spend shopping for Staging essentials, and the time it takes you to assemble your team, load your car or truck with supplies, unload it, and then de-Stage the project once the house is sold. After you have priced a few projects, you will get a much better sense of how to bid. Most beginning Stagers underestimate all these factors and underbid their first few projects. Doing so is a healthy learning experience— don't beat yourself up about it; it happens to all of us.

I do not recommend changing the price. Stick to the bid you gave the homeowners originally. It is not their responsibility to pay for your miscalculation, and it's unprofessional to come back to them halfway through the project with a weak explanation: "I missed the mark and didn't charge enough. Sorry . . ."

The average ASP Home Stager charges $75 to $100 an hour, although some charge $150 or more and others as little as $50, depending on their level of expertise and where they live in the country. These rates are internal ones for the most part, used to calculate consultations and bids.

When you set your fees, think about how much money you will need to keep your business going. Consider how much it costs per month to run your office, cover overhead (insurance, legal/accounting fees, utilities, gasoline), pay your taxes, and also pay anyone who assists you. This is not hard to do. Make a list and add it up. For example:

- Computer (hardware and software purchases; amortize over a 12-month period).
- Technical support.
- Internet access.

- Telephone.
- Other utilities (electric, heat, air-conditioning).
- Office supplies.
- Staging supplies.
- Insurance (divide annual premiums by 12).
- Taxes (check with your accountant).
- Inventory (set aside a monthly amount to build inventory).
- Professional dues.
- Advertising and marketing expenses.
- The cost of paying other Stagers.

Notice anything missing from this list? Only the most important line item: you!

If you are able to run your business on a break-even basis for a few months or longer, you only need to bring in enough to meet the monthly expenses such as those in the preceding list. If you must earn more so that you can pay your own mortgage and buy your kids new shoes, you will have to decide how much you need and set your sights accordingly. Here are some examples of income streams using simple math:

Staging Business with a Moderate Level of Activity

- Stage four properties a month for $1,500 each = $6,000.
- Consult on two properties a month for $375 each = $750.
- Total for one month = $6,750.
- Total gross for the year, based on these figures = $81,000.

If you want to work less, then divide these figures in half and you will still gross about $40,000 a year.

Staging Business with a High Level of Activity

- Stage five properties a month for $1,500 each = $7,500.
- Consult on six properties a month for $375 each = $2,250.

- Total for one month: $9,750.
- Total gross for the year, based on these figures: $117,000.

If you want to make more money, multiply these figures by 2. This will mean you need to Stage perhaps 10 properties a month and complete 12 consultations a month. If you do, you could gross more than $234,000 a year.

Remember, these are *gross* figures—not income in your pocket (you have to deduct your expenses to determine your net earnings), but these examples can give you a good idea of how much potential there is once you become a Stager. If you become an ASP Stager, the potential is even greater because you have access to the repository of information, knowledge, and experience that I and my company, StagedHomes.com, can offer.

I believe it is everyone's dream to do something they love and be paid well for it. The Home Staging industry, which I invented, nurtured, and worked hard to build, is a field that many women and men are entering in order to fulfill this dream. When you Stage homes creatively for the good of all those involved, you will be doing what you love and earning money, too. Follow your dream and make it happen!

CHAPTER 7

MARKETING YOUR HOME STAGING BUSINESS

The way you live in your home is not how you market your house.
—BARB SCHWARZ

Marketing your business is essential for success. Actually, marketing is *mandatory* for success. You might have the most creative Staging ideas and you may be able to convert the most troublesome house into a buyer's dream, but if no one knows about you, you will never be able to demonstrate your gift and build a business around it. Most businesses fail because of inadequate marketing, and a Home Staging business is no exception. The sad truth is that unless you are able to get out and talk to people effectively, network, and sell yourself and your business, you simply will not achieve the success you deserve, no matter how terrific a Stager you are.

When you decide to start your own Staging business, there are two markets you need to reach: the real estate market and the general public. The former is targeted and quantifiable, and might have a degree of understanding about Staging. The latter is hard to define or pin down, and, when it comes to Staging, is most likely unaware of the industry's significance and value.

A good marketing plan will allow you to reach both targets to get your message out to the community—loud and clear.

THE MARKETING PLAN

Like the business plan you wrote when you launched your Home Staging business, the marketing plan is a road map to help you navigate your way into the marketplace. The plan should be clear and specific. Give yourself reasonable goals and deadlines. I will expand on these later in this chapter, but in a nutshell, here is what your marketing plan should include:

- Plan to set up one-on-one meetings with every real estate office in town. Arrange for a meeting with the broker/ manager and also with individual agents. When you are just starting out, you might want to set a goal to schedule, say, two or three of these meetings a week. Another goal could be to give a presentation on Home Staging to a real estate office once a week.

- List the professional associations you plan to join. Make a commitment to join all of them by a date in the not-too-distant future. Your priority should be to join the local real estate associations as an affiliate member so that you can meet and network with the agents in your area. I find the Women's Council of Realtors (WCR) very valuable, too. In addition, become a member of the chamber of commerce, Rotary Club, Lions Club, builder associations such as Business Network International (BNI), the Soroptimists (an international humanitarian association for women in management and the professions), and the local garden club or women's club. These organizations will bring you into the community and the real estate markets in ways you have never before experienced.

- Include a plan to interact with the media. Write a clear, short press release to send to local newspapers and magazines. (For ASPs, I have written a press release on the Staging University that they can use immediately upon graduation from the ASP Staging course). Keep it brief; it's not a novel. If you are unsure how to do this, look for samples of press releases online or in books. Remember to find out the name of the appropriate editor (home, business, real estate, etc.) at the publication and address it to him or her. Send a different press release every month to keep your name in front of the media. Eventually, someone will put you in the paper or local lifestyle magazine and may even call upon you as an expert. Keep a positive attitude. Newspapers and other media need to fill pages and airwaves, and they look for press releases to help them do it. It's only a matter of time before this strategy works.

- Identify local homeowners' and builders' associations. Target them for presentations. Remember, every homeowner buys or sells a house at some point (and they have neighbors and friends). Builders are in the business of building and selling houses, and they need your services, too. I predict that we will see more builder's homes being Staged in the future and fewer model homes, which tend to be decorated so that buyers cannot see what they are getting. Home Staging for new construction is already happening and will continue to grow as a trend. Talk to local builders, show them your Career Book, and give them a presentation, and I suspect you will be solidly on your way to Staging their new houses.

- Practice describing your business in a professional way. You need to be comfortable selling yourself and your business, whether you have 10 seconds, one minute, five minutes, or an hour. All of these time frames are important, so practice until you are competent in each.

One of the best business ideas I have developed is to say to a prospective client, "Let me tell you how I work." If you describe your process to potential customers, no one else will do it for you. When you educate potential clients, use this statement to initiate the discussion.

- Offer to make a presentation about Staging for one of the local clubs you have joined. You never know who might be impressed by your winning personality and first-rate business sense when they hear you talk about the magic of Home Staging and all the great things it does for homeowners and buyers.

As with any business or product, word of mouth is your best friend. There is no substitute for getting your face in front of the largest number of people you can. The more people who see you, listen to you, and begin to understand your work and our industry, the more business you will have. Get out there and market yourself!

HOW TO BRAND YOUR BUSINESS

Branding is an integral part of marketing, and I recommend that you make the effort to brand your business.

Before you throw up your hands in frustration and exclaim, "I know nothing about branding! Gosh, Barb, isn't there enough to do already?" take a moment to grasp this concept. It is worth your time.

Put simply, your brand is your promise to your clients. It is intangible and future oriented, and yet it communicates to them that your company can meet a need or solve a problem. It is a confirmation of your values, manifested by your attitude, your commitment, and, eventually, your reputation. Perhaps most important, your brand must be reflected in everything you say and do.

Although a brand is *not* a logo, a slogan, or an advertisement, your logo or slogan should demonstrate your brand—and through a logo or slogan you must remind clients of your commitment to them. This is part of the branding process.

For instance, a homeowner who considers hiring you should think: "When I hire this person to Stage my property, I will make a smart investment in my financial well-being." Because of your brand, you can authenticate your promise to the customer to do the best, most professional job possible.

Good branding immediately makes it clear that you stand head and shoulders above the competition. It delivers an obvious message, adds to your credibility, and promotes loyalty with clients.

As you recall, Chapter 1 explained that a successful business meets challenges and creates solutions for its customers. Your brand will communicate to your clients that your business is in existence expressly to address any number of challenges for them.

There are several ways to brand your company. Turn back to Chapter 3 and review the importance of a mission statement. When your mission statement is crystal clear, you have nearly accomplished the branding of your company. Physical manifestations of your brand appear in your Career Book, which you leave with your clients and which needs to include your mission statement. You also need to come up with a good name, an uncomplicated but effective logo, and a tagline that tells prospective customers exactly what you do. Once you have these in place, your job is to integrate your brand into every aspect of your business. This means your company name and logo should appear on every communication and piece of equipment you have, as much as possible. An effective brand will stay with the customer, as well as your smile and professionalism.

Do not listen to the naysayers who scoff at the idea of branding a small business. It's just as critical for a small business as it is for a large one. You can create your own brand or you can hire a professional to help you brand your business. Believe it or not, there are firms that specialize in branding. However, you can learn a lot from web sites and books about effective branding, and if you are an ASP Stager, you can visit StagedHomes.com and learn even more.

As the creator of Home Staging, I have worked to set standards, guidelines, policies, procedures, and practices for the industry I invented. I thought, "If I do not do this, then who will?" As an educator and business leader, I feel very good about where we have arrived and where we are going. I will continue to build the industry so that it reaches its full potential. To help me accomplish this, I established the ASP and the ASPM designations and certification processes. The ASP designation is a brand, and yet I feel it is more than that. Those who become an ASP or ASPM understand the responsibility they have to live up to the standards I have established for the Home Staging industry.

To learn how to become an ASP or an ASPM, please see the box at the end of this chapter.

YOUR CAREER BOOK

I devised the concept of the Career Book many years ago to build my credibility with clients. Today it is more vital than ever to rely on an outstanding Career Book. I refer to the Career Book often and have described it briefly several times. Because it is such an important part of marketing your business, I will explain it in more detail here.

This is your personal marketing system that sells *you* in a thoughtful and understated way. It is designed to be left with potential clients so that they can learn about you at their leisure. When a customer or real estate agent looks though the book, it builds trust in you and your services. In some ways, it's an expanded resume and will help you establish and maintain rapport and credibility with a wide range of people. Your Career Book is also part of your branding strategy.

Make sure the pages of the Career Book are logically organized and look attractive and enticing—let your inner graphic designer come into play here! The book should look snappy and fresh, never tired or dog-eared. Update the photos and references regularly. I like to include a few personal items, as well, to help me stand out as an individual. For me, this means pictures of my family and my pets and mention of my hobbies. For you, it could be a photo of your family or your garden or something else you identify with. Clients respond to personal information because they like to do business with real people. People buy people, and so to establish trust, sprinkle a little of yourself in the Career Book.

The Career Book does the talking for you. Make sure it is more of a picture book than a collection of long articles about Staging, real estate, or you. People love to look at photographs, and they like to read brief testimonials from former customers and letters of recommendation.

Your Career Book is about your career, so fill it with information that establishes your credibility. You can reference past careers and include your ASP certification, and before-and-after pictures from houses you have Staged. Over the years, I have asked ASP Stagers if I could buy their Career Books from them. They turn me down every time. "Are you kidding?" they say. "This is the best and easiest way to establish my credibility. People believe in me once they see it and it brings me more business than anything I have ever done."

Career Books work!

HOW TO MARKET TO THE REAL ESTATE COMMUNITY

A great deal of your business will come from real estate agents and brokers. I will say it again: Staging is part of the real estate industry, not the decorating industry. As Stagers, we help homeowners sell their houses or condominiums for top dollar by preparing them for sale. It stands to reason that real estate professionals will be the ones to request our services for their clients.

This is changing, and I couldn't be happier. Today, an increasing number of homeowners are hiring Stagers before they list their houses. This represents a big step forward for our industry. It is a huge paradigm shift, and one that I predicted more than 10 years ago. Although the day has not arrived when every seller automatically calls a Stager, it is happening more often than ever before. This is because of articles about the real estate business in newspapers and magazines and on web sites, television shows, and radio programs. And it's due to word of mouth. People are talking about Staging.

I have spoken to more than a million real estate professionals across North America, teaching them all I know about Staging and convincing them that it works. You can't educate that many individuals about something so meaningful and not expect the word to spread.

Because of this reality, you, as a Stager, must educate the real estate community about Staging in general and let them know about your business specifically. Ideally, you need to be part of the agent's marketing plan, part of the team. You need to give every real estate professional you meet your business card and your brochure, show them your Career Book, and discuss the Staging successes you have had. Chapter 8 explains how to build and maintain your relationships with the real estate community.

When you start your company, make a list of the real estate agencies you want to work with and set up appointments to meet with the principals. Drive through neighborhoods in your town and make note of the real estate company signs in front yards and the names of the brokers attached to them. Peruse the local newspapers for real estate advertisements and add names to your target list from them. Go on local company web sites and add the names of the company's agents to your list.

Look for designations after the real estate agents' names and start by contacting anyone with the most designations. These are the agents who have been in business for a while and are serious enough about their careers to continue their education. For instance, within the Realtor designation are about a dozen special designations, such as Accredited Buyer Representative (ABR) and Certified Residential Specialist (CRS).

Agents generally are independent salespeople who work under the supervision of the broker, who represents the company. Some brokers work in management and some work as agents; brokers have more experience and education than agents. I know this can be confusing, but if you are going to work in the real estate industry you need to understand who the players are and how they interact. Become an affiliate member of the local board of Realtors, which will also help you navigate these waters. The important thing is to meet as many people in the real estate business as you can and tell them what you do and how your services can help them.

Start with the owner or manager of the company. Depending on whether the real estate company is independently owned or part of a franchise or chain, this person may or may not be one and the same. Once you meet with the person, ask to meet with individual brokers and agents. The more people you can meet one-on-one, the better.

I find it's a good idea to stop by the office and set up an appointment with the sales manager. Even if the manager is unavailable, you can establish rapport with the administrative assistant or receptionist and leave your Career Book for the office staff to look at. Remember that these people very powerful in a real estate office. You can approach them with a small token such as a box of candy, as well as a big smile, and you will make an influential friend who will enjoy looking through your Career Book. Ask the administrative assistant or receptionist to promise to show it to the manager. When you pick up the book on another day, you never know who might want to meet you as a result. I have been recognized when I walked through the door: "Aren't you Barb who left the Career Book here the other day?" It is an effective way to sell yourself.

Once you get your foot in the door, offer to make a presentation for the entire office. Explain that this will be an educational experience. You are looking for work, of course, but you realize that the more real estate pros know about Staging, the greater the chance you will get a referral. Don't assume that the agents and managers understand what Staging is. Perhaps they have heard of it and have some idea what it is, but they also will have misconceptions and a general lack of knowledge, especially if Staging is a fairly new concept in your market area. Look at this as an opportunity to educate some very prominent people.

Whether your presentation is five minutes or one hour long, your main role is to educate real estate agents and managers in four specific ways:

1. To explain what Staging truly is and what it is not.
2. To show how Staging can help real estate agents list and sell more homes faster or for more money, or both.
3. To provide agents with tips and Staging ideas that they can use to educate sellers.
4. To describe how you, as a Staging professional, work.

When you give the presentation, bring your Career Book, your business cards, brochures, before-and-after pictures from a couple of your Staging projects, and a handout for each person in attendance. Light refreshments are a good idea, too. I always say that the way to the an agent's heart is through his or her stomach!

During your presentation or a one-on-one meeting, you may hear that a particular company or agent already works with a Stager. If this happens, do not say, "Oh, gee, thanks for your time. Goodbye." No! Instead, say, "That's fantastic! I am so glad you appreciate the value of Staging. I understand you are loyal to the Stager you already work with, but please keep my card anyway." With a broad smile on your face, ask the person to call you "in case you have the need for my services at any time in the future." Leave your Career Book with the agent, too. Offer a gift certificate for a complimentary consultation or one-room Staging. The gift certificates are easy to make on the computer—be sure to include your contact information and the name of your company. When anyone in the real estate company needs a Stager and their regular is booked, you can bet that they will call you.

You can develop a mutually beneficial relationship by offering discounted group rates for consultations to real estate agents who send a lot of business your way. This would work particularly well with agents who decide to include your services as part of their marketing plans. For example, if your average consultation is $450, you might charge the agent $400. You will make up the $50 loss in no time with the extra volume and in consultations that turn into Stagings. Agents will love the idea, and it could end up paying off for you as well.

HOW TO MARKET TO THE PUBLIC

As I mentioned, one of my favorite predictions is that before long, John Q. and Jane Public will call Stagers directly, rather than going through real estate professionals. I already see this happening across the country. Rarely do I give an ASP Staging course that someone does not tell me about an instance where a home seller has contacted a Stager, sometimes even before calling a listing agent.

I can't tell you how gratifying this is to hear! Staging really is changing the home-selling business—and for the better. Homeowners are taking charge of their properties and making sure they get the highest price they can. I say, "Hooray!"

This is extremely reassuring. When you start a Home Staging business, you should market your services directly to the public as well as to the real estate community. Doing so takes some effort, but if you are secure in your brand, you will convey to anyone who listens to you that you are a consummate professional who will do nothing short of a spectacular job for your client.

Once you have joined the local organizations I suggested earlier in this chapter, you can begin to market yourself by offering to make presentations about Staging to these organizations. Many of these clubs are happy to schedule a talk for their monthly meetings and nearly everyone who owns a house loves to learn about real estate. Your talk will probably bring in a good crowd. This is as true for the Rotary Club as it is for the local garden club.

Contact the local newspaper, radio station, and television station. If you write well, offer to provide an article or a series of articles on Staging for selling homes. If you don't want to write articles, send the features editor (or home, garden, or real estate editor) press releases about your business and your goals. The editor just might assign a reporter to write a story about you.

Bring ideas to the radio and television stations, too. People who produce talk shows may ask you to be a guest if your ideas are educational enough. No show wants to book anyone who is simply promoting a business.

Never give up on the media. They should be part of your marketing plan. Establish relationships with anyone you meet who has ties to the newspaper or radio or TV station. Even when you get busy, don't forget about them. They can be your best friends when your business slows down a little or when you want to expand.

Approach homeowners' and builders' associations. Offer to make a presentation to them. Talk to Welcome Wagon or a similar organization about offering your shopping services to new residents. Some folks may also want to hire you to Stage their new houses—what I call *Staging to Live*. I really believe that in a few years you will hear more and more about Staging to Live rather than decorating. When most people think of decorating, they think of spending money; Staging to Live does not cost much, since, like Staging to Sell, the Stager relies mainly on the furniture and accessories the homeowner already possesses. Who wouldn't love this concept?

HOW TO GIVE A PRESENTATION ON STAGING

I have mentioned several times that it's a good idea to give a presentation on Staging to real estate professionals as well as to the public through organizations such as the Rotary Club and women's clubs. When you have taken my three-day ASP course, you will have an inkling of what goes into a presentation, although what I do in those three days is far more extensive than what you will do in a single lecture.

Before I describe what goes into the presentation, I want to recommend that you join Toastmasters—unless you are already a skillful public speaker. Toastmasters gives you the opportunity to practice speaking in front of an audience, and you learn a lot of useful tips at the same time. The more relaxed you are as a public speaker, the better your presentations will be.

Keep the presentation to about 45 minutes. This will allow 15 minutes for questions at the end, if you are allotted an hour for the meeting. If the real estate company or organization asks you to make the talk shorter, accommodate them.

Divide the presentation into three parts:

1. Describe the benefits of Staging. If you are an ASP Stager, use statistics from our web site, StagedHomes.com. Explain that Staging is a value-added service and that most homes sell more quickly for a better price than those that are not Staged. Be sure to tell your audience that an investment in Staging costs less than the seller's first price reduction. Wow

them, too, with before-and-after pictures. If you don't have many pictures, try Staging your own or your neighbor's house to get pictures of your work. ASP Stagers can take pictures from my web site. I use PowerPoint when I give a presentation, and I suggest you learn how to do this. It's very easy and very effective. One word of warning: Don't mention the names or addresses of clients when you show these pictures. You must protect their privacy. When properties sell, the details are public knowledge, as the sale is recorded by the municipality or county and anyone can look up information about the sale. Nevertheless, it's good business to be discreet.

2. Provide information about how to Stage. This is when you can give tips for decluttering, for arranging furniture, and for sprucing up the outside of a house. I suggest you talk about Barb's Three C's of Staging: clean, clutterfree, and color (more about these in Chapter 9).

3. Talk about you. This is where you can explain how you work, that you do everything according to a step-by-step process, and that you are available for consultations (for which you charge) and for bids. Don't give flat figures, but provide price ranges and time estimates so that your audience gets a good idea of what is involved. Use words such as "average" and "in general." If you are quizzed aggressively by someone in the crowd, make it clear that you will be happy to talk specific pricing with him or her after the presentation or whenever the person wants to make an appointment. Let everyone know you are willing to prepare bids for no initial investment.

Make sure you have plenty of business cards, postcards, brochures, or anything else you can pass out to the audience. If it's appropriate, supply snacks; nothing draws people in as much as food. Of course, when you finish your talk, make sure you pack up any equipment, visual aids, and food you have brought along.

If you are enthusiastic and excited about Staging, your audience will pick up on your zeal. You won't have time to share everything, but even if you did, it's best to leave them wanting to hear more. You will be invited back for another presentation, which is what you want.

BARB'S SPEAKING TIPS

I have been speaking in front of audiences for more than 20 years. As you know from the introduction to this book, I gave up selling and Staging houses in 1985, when I was approached by a real estate promoter to talk about Staging to real estate professionals all across the country. At the time, Staging was a brand-new concept, and as its creator, I was the logical person to spread the word. I knew this was something I was meant to do!

For the next 13 years, I was on the road for 40 weeks of the year and addressed more than a million people in that time. When I was younger, I had been interested in musical theater and performing; I was never what you would call a shrinking violet. Still, I had to learn a lot about public speaking, and today, as a motivational speaker and seminar leader, I am completely at ease in front of an audience. You could say I am at my happiest and most energized when I can stand up and teach others about the subject about which I am so passionate. I have now logged more than 17,000 hours speaking about Home Staging across the United States and Canada.

I mentioned earlier in this chapter that it's a great idea to join Toastmasters to learn to be at ease when speaking in front of people. Some of us are born hams (I should know!), but most of us are not. Even if you feel confident, here are some tips that will make you a better speaker:

- Practice, practice, practice. This is not just the way to get to Carnegie Hall, but also the way to be an effective public speaker. Join Toastmasters, as I mentioned, but also find someone to practice in front of before you give your talk. Print your outline and keep it with you as you go about your daily business. Keep thinking about your presentation and reciting what you will say. Once you are used to hearing the words come out of your mouth, they will flow naturally when you make the presentation. You cannot practice too much!

- Speak freely. Although I have just urged you to practice, practice, practice, try not to sound too rehearsed and do not read from notes. Use an outline and highlight items that will trigger the points you want to make.

- Be happy. Everyone responds to excitement. If you feel happy, you need to notify your face. Smile! Most of us who become Home Stagers are so passionate about Staging that good energy flows naturally. Practice sharing your passion, too. People love to be with others who believe in what they are doing. Don't be afraid to let your excitement show. Speak with happy enthusiasm.

- Read your audience. Feel the room. Is it too hot or cold? Are there distractions? Maintain control as well as you can. If you are volunteering your time to a real estate office, make sure the agents are giving you their time, too. Watch the expressions on the faces of your audience. If you see you are losing their attention, move on and mix things up to inject some variety into your talk. If you are talking to real estate agents, remember that they don't want a lecture; they want to know what is in it for them when it comes to Staging. It's your job to help them understand why they should include a Stager as a standard part of their services. They want to know how it will improve their bottom line.

- Remember that when you are speaking to any audience, you represent our new and growing industry. Maintain your enthusiasm for the subject, and never waver in your professionalism. For the sake of all of us, put your best foot forward. You cannot sell if you are not sold.

- Finally, dress for the occasion. We are in the business of making our clients' homes look good, so dress with style and flair. If you have a name tag, wear it. It will reinforce who you are to the audience. Stage everything you do. Stage the food for the presentation. Stage the presentation. Stage the car you arrive in. Stage yourself.

HOW TO MAKE THE BEST USE OF THE INTERNET

It's a good idea to have your own web site. Businesspeople and the general public expect it more and more every day. My company, StagedHomes.com, hosts feature pages for all ASPs, which serve as mini web sites within our overall web site. Our ASPM Master graduates receive three web pages. When you start a web site, think of it as a window into your business. It should be inviting, warm, and professional, with user-friendly buttons and drop-down menus.

Your site does not need to be complex, but it does need to be clear and simple to navigate. Load as many before-and-after photos as you can—everyone loves these—and provide a short explanation of what you did to Stage a particular room or outside area. Use your own pictures and do not take any from other web sites. Not only is it not ethical, but it could come back to bite you in a big way. As with the photographs for your Career Book and the web site, be sure never to identify the home or the homeowner.

Include a short biography of yourself or an explanation of why you are a Home Stager. Put your mission statement on your web site. Explain how you work, but don't provide exact prices or fees. If anyone sends you a complimentary note or e-mail, ask permission to use it on the site as a testimonial to your good work.

Finally, be sure to include a way for site visitors to reach you. This is the "contact us" button. When they hit it, not only should visitors get an e-mail address or window, they should also be able to find your telephone number easily.

Include your web address on all your literature and expect interested people to visit the site. This can happen in the middle of the night, on Sundays, and on holidays, so be sure to keep your site up and running, without glitches. Nothing is more frustrating for a potential client than to visit a site and find that the applications do not function. You may be able to maintain the site yourself, or you might prefer to hire a webmaster.

Web sites are wonderful. They make you look professional and they can bring you lots of business, but they also can get lost in the infinity of the Internet if they are not optimized so that they can be found by the search engines. Web site optimization is a part of the high-tech industry that many don't know about, but if you want to be found, it is crucial. Optimizing your site does not need to be expensive. If you want your web site to be successful, make sure you investigate how to do it. A good place to start is to type the words "how to optimize a web site" into Google or Yahoo and visit the sites that offer help.

TRADE SHOWS

Whenever possible, attend trade shows. These might be home shows, builders' expos, property trade fairs, or even garden shows. As you can afford it and it makes sense, rent space and set up a booth, or team up with other Stagers or a real estate company to share a booth. Our ASP Stagers get together all the time to share booth space. Doing so is a good way to save money.

Every show attracts a different group of attendees, and the trick is selecting shows that provide you with the right exposure. Quality is key here. The attendees' profile should match that of your prospective customer or real estate client. When you are new to the Staging business world, you might want to go to shows as an attendee to get a sense of what they offer and whom they attract.

When you decide on a show you want to participate in with a booth, coordinate preshow promotion so that your customers and other contacts know you will be there. This will bring people to your booth; to attract more visitors, consider an incentive, such as a drawing for a complimentary Home Staging consultation. When the show has door prizes, offer your services as one of them. If the show has demonstrations or lectures, arrange to give a Staging presentation. You might be able to barter these things as a way to reduce the cost of the booth.

Be sure to Stage your booth. Use furniture, plants, and accessories to make it stand out from the rest. Keep signs easy to see and comprehend. Provide attractive brochures and make sure you have enough on hand. Ask customers to sign a guest book or leave a business card so you can gather names and addresses. Add them to your contact list and mail them additional information after the show.

Take advantage of the networking opportunities of a show. Make sure that you walk the convention floor and meet anyone who might help you build business.

When the show is over, follow up with everyone who demonstrated interest in your services. Plans for how you will accomplish this should be in place long before the show opens, so that you can implement them quickly. Any lead can turn into business, and yet without efficient nurturing, any lead can also turn cold.

After you have tested the waters with your marketing plan, you are going to have to maintain the relationships you have cultivated. At this point in time, the most valuable are those you have with real estate professionals. In Chapter 8, I explain how to work with them to get the biggest results for your effort.

THE ASP BRAND

The ASP brand is the number one Home Staging designation and brand in the United States and Canada. It exemplifies what branding is all about. The media have recognized the ASP brand for its standards of excellence, training, and service, and the professionalism that ASPs stand for and deliver to the public and the real estate industry. "Together we can accomplish anything and together we accomplish everything!" is my motto, which expresses what I believe about the ASP designation. In the world of Home Staging, more ASPs mean more business for all ASPs. The word is out and the brand is working. We are delivering great service to all those with whom we work.

The word that comes to mind when people think about the ASPs they know is *heart*. ASPs are known for caring deeply about the clients whom they serve and for bringing about the greatest good for all.

HOW TO BECOME AN ASP OR ASPM STAGER

When you successfully complete my three-day ASP Staging course, you are awarded the ASP designation. When you complete my five-day master's program, you become an ASP Master Stager (ASPM). Think of these designations as solid gold! Not only can you put the designation after your name, but you can take advantage of all the support my company, StagedHomes.com, provides.

Here are the high points:

- You will receive your own feature page as an ASP Home Stager. This is a personalized mini web site hosted by my larger site. You can refer clients to your web page, where they can read about you and view photos of the houses you have Staged. We have made it easy for you to display all the before-and-after pictures you desire, and if you need it, we have excellent technical support. We also have audio capability so you can add your own message or testimonial.

- As an ASP or ASPM, you have the resources of the online Staging University available to you. There are literally thousands of pages and pictures for you to access and use, offering forms, marketing ideas, Staging ideas, and so much more. Home Stagers say the university is an important part of being an ASP.

- As an ASP Stager, you receive a customized Career Book as part of your registration. It consists of top-of-the-line materials and will last for years. When you assemble yours, include everything that you deem will educate customers and real estate agents about you and your Staging business. This might include your mission statement, your biography, your code of ethics (all ASP Stagers follow a strict code, as detailed on page 19), and a list of references. The book should also have as many before-and-after pictures as you think necessary to demonstrate your abilities and talent.

- You can use any of the Staging tools I have created with the ASP logo to market your business. These include yard signs (similar to those used by real estate agents), doormats, car magnets, license plate holders, business card stickers and business card holders, tote bags, lightweight jackets, polo shirts, ASP labels, and ASP Master Post-its.

(continued)

- There are any number of opportunities to network with other ASP Stagers and ASP Real Estate Agents. This can help you find work in your neck of the woods. You can also share Staging and marketing ideas that have worked—and a few that have not!
- You can join one of our IAHSP ASP chapters and get a fast start building your business by assisting other ASPs and working together in teams, should you decide to take advantage of this wonderful opportunity. There are thousands of ASPs in cities and towns across the United States and Canada.
- I have established affiliations with national companies that give discounts to our ASPs and their customers. This means you can provide even better service to your clients.
- And more—I am always adding new services for our ASPs. Sponsors and vendors recognize that we are the leaders in the Home Staging industry, and they are interested in serving those we serve as ASPs and ASPMs, which in turn serves the public.
- To learn more about becoming an ASP Stager go to www.StagedHomes.com.

CHAPTER 8

HOW TO WORK WITH REAL ESTATE PROFESSIONALS

Detail your house like you detail your car!
—BARB SCHWARZ

As you begin your Home Staging career, you may find that much of your work comes from the real estate community. As your business grows and word of mouth spreads from seller to seller, you may, in time, rely less on local real estate agents and more on other kinds of referrals. This is wonderful and gratifying, but because Staging is part of the real estate industry, it always will work in tandem with it.

Staged homes sell faster and for more money than those that are not Staged. This means that our business affects a lot of people: sellers, listing real estate agents, buyers, mortgage brokers, neighbors,

117

Stagers (you), vendors, and miscellaneous suppliers. How is that for a ripple effect!

As increasing numbers of real estate agents and brokers come to believe in the value of Staging, it will assume a prominent role in the house-selling business. It's your job—and I am sure you will find that it is also your joy—to educate them. As you know, one of my favorite axioms is: "The investment of Staging in your home is less than a price reduction on your home!" I reword this slightly when I talk to real estate agents: "The investment of Staging in your listings is less than a price reduction on your listings." Why does this also hold true for real estate agents? Because agents earn a percentage of the selling price, so the lower the selling price, the lower the agent's fee. This is exactly the kind of realism that real estate agents love. And who can blame them?

For these and other reasons, it's vital that you establish and nurture relationships with real estate agents and brokers.

STARTING A RELATIONSHIP WITH THE REAL ESTATE COMMUNITY

When you decide to open your business, make a list of all the real estate agencies in town or in your section of the city. Include small and independent agencies as well as large franchises. Your list could be a long one and because your marketing plan directs you to call on a certain number of agencies a week (see Chapter 7), you might be at sea about where to begin. Don't go canoeing without a paddle! Start with those you know: the agency that sold you your house (if the experience was good), an agency where you know someone, or the agency with so many advertisements that you can't ignore them. Drive through neighborhoods that appeal to you. Jot down the names of the individual agents posted on the For Sale signs and make a note of the affiliated real estate agencies.

Once you have a list, start making calls. Chapter 7 explains how to find the names of the owners and managers of the real estate companies by visiting their web sites or calling the office and asking outright. Make appointments with these people. When you get them on the telephone, explain that you are a Home Stager (if you are an ASP Stager, all the better—it's an accomplishment; boast about it!) and that you would like a few minutes of their time to tell them about your business and discuss ways you could help theirs.

My mantra is: Never take no for an answer! If you feel you are not getting anywhere with the owner or manager, stop by the office and chat up the administrative assistant or receptionist. It's no secret that I believe the best way to get in the door is to actually walk through it. It's tougher to give you the brush-off when you are standing there in person. Leave your Career Book, as well as a few business cards and brochures, if you have them. Come back the next day to pick up the Career Book and don't be surprised if it's now easy to schedule appointments with the owner, manager, and a few brokers and agents. As Chapter 7 makes clear, the Career Book is an effective marketing tool.

When you sit down with the agency's principals—the owner, managing broker, designated broker, or sales manager—be direct and professional. Real estate professionals might already know what you can do for them, but do not assume that they do. No one knows what they want until you tell them. Build a rapport with them even as you educate them. Use statistics from this book or from StagedHomes.com to demonstrate how well Staged homes sell. Use a few of the key phrases from the following list to get your points across and get the conversation going:

- "The investment of staging in your property is less than a price reduction on your property."
- "The way you live in your home and the way you sell your house are two different things."
- "You can't sell it if you can't see it."
- "If you can smell it, you can't sell it."

- "Buyers only know what they see, not the way it's going to be."
- "Staging is not condition."
- "The same person who would never sell his car without detailing it should not sell his home without Staging it."
- "Detail your house like you detail your car . . . we call it Staging!"
- "When it comes to Staging, less is more."

Once you have a meeting or two with people at a particular real estate agency, offer to give a presentation for the entire office. Refer to Chapter 7 for tips on giving presentations. When you are adequately prepared and pace the presentation properly, you will have a standing-room-only crowd! Why? Everyone loves the idea of Staging because, let's face it, everyone loves before-and-after pictures of just about anything, and nothing fascinates people more than looking at other people's houses. Real estate professionals are no exception. What's more, these men and women have seen it all—filthy kitchens, trash-strewn basements, piles of newspapers stacked to the ceiling, mold on the walls, and the most hideous wallpaper ever designed. Once you swap a few war stories with them, they will pick up on your enthusiasm and your presentation will be a big success.

Of course, the purpose of the presentation is to educate real estate agents about the value of Staging. If you can convince them that when they Stage their properties they will sell listings faster and for more money, you will have them in the palm of your hand.

During the presentation or in one-on-one meetings, agents will ask you how they should present the idea of Staging to their customers. Suggest that they use a few of the key phrases listed previously and mentioned throughout this book. Sellers are generally reassured to hear that Staging is only temporary and is a tool to sell the property quickly and for top dollar. Emphasize that Staging is not decorating and thus has nothing to do with the sellers' personal taste, which will strike a chord with the agents. It means that they do not have to like or work with the homeowners' taste because when the clients Stage, the house is depersonalized. Staging is a way to make the house or condominium appeal to the broadest range of buyers—nothing more and nothing less.

MAINTAINING AND EXPANDING YOUR RELATIONSHIP WITH THE REAL ESTATE COMMUNITY

Once you have one real estate office on board and ready to call you for Staging projects, move on to the next. I don't advise that you establish an exclusive arrangement with a single agency. Other businesses that serve the real estate market rarely team with only one agency, and neither should you. Mortgage companies, appraisers, and home inspectors work for everyone in town and rely on their own reputations and individual relationships to keep their phones ringing. As a Stager, you are in the same category.

When you find a group of agents you hit it off with, offer to contribute to their newsletter or run a joint ad campaign with them. Suggest an advertisement for a Staged Home of the Week or an ad with bragging rights on houses that have sold as a result of Staging.

Don't neglect those agents you have met once or twice but who have never asked you to Stage one of their properties. Send them a monthly newsletter to keep your name in front of them. If you are mentioned in the newspaper or are scheduled to appear on a television or radio show, send a broadcast e-mail to your entire real estate mailing list. Send postcards regularly and announce your latest Staged property. Real estate agents most likely will know the house and recall how quickly it sold—and for what price. They'll be impressed! Keep track of how long it's been between presentations at each real estate office with which you've established a relationship. If it's been more than five or six months, offer to give another presentation. Assure the manager that you have new material.

As Chapter 7 suggests, visit public open houses on weekends and leave your business card. If there are no buyers at the open house, talk with the agent on the premises. With no one else around, you can speak freely and get to know the agent. You could even walk through a few rooms and make some Staging suggestions. If you impress the agent, he or she might hire you on the spot or call you in a day or two.

Do the same during broker open house tours. These are usually scheduled during the week, when most agents from the local offices drive from new listing to new listing and walk through the houses. You can go on these tours. Ask an agent you know to take you along. This is an exceedingly good way to meet a wide spectrum of the people involved in the local real estate industry, including home inspectors and bankers, who also go on broker tours. These tours are great opportunities to network with all these people and perhaps pick up some referrals. Introduce yourself to everyone; you never know who might refer you for a Staging project. Try to ride with a different agent on each trip between houses; chat about Staging possibilities in a low-key way and work on establishing a friendly, businesslike rapport with the agents. This is not the time for a hard sell. Be yourself, be friendly and positive, and share the joy and advantages of Home Staging wherever you go and whenever the opportunity arises.

Here are some surefire tips for establishing, maintaining, and building relationships with the real estate companies in your area:

- Always know the names of an agency's owner/manager and sales manager before you call for an appointment. These are easy to find on company web sites.

- Arrange for one-on-one introductory meetings with as many people in the real estate industry as you can.
- In each introductory meeting, explain Staging as concisely as you can. Start by saying, as I do, "Let me tell you how I work." Leave your card, brochure, and Career Book at the agency.
- If you don't get an appointment over the phone, visit the agency and leave your Career Book, business cards, and brochure with the administrative assistant or receptionist. This might be a better strategy in the long run. Most of us are more effective in person than on the telephone, and, likewise, we have more control of the situation in person.
- Give each agent a little gift—for example, a small terra-cotta pot containing a seed packet and a card that says: "I want to help you grow your business through the magic of Staging your listings!" Or drop off a jar of jelly beans with a card that says: "Sales of your listings *"bean"* slow lately? Stage your listings to sell now!" Use your imagination to come up with other attention-grabbing ideas.
- Offer to give a presentation about Staging to the office.
- Go on the broker tours during the week to see the latest real estate listings.
- On weekends, go to public open houses. Talk to the agent at each house, explaining the service you perform through your Staging work. If the agent is busy with a potential buyer, do not interrupt. When the agent is free, introduce yourself and explain what you do.
- Leave your business cards and brochures wherever you can.
- When you are first starting out, offer free consultations or Stagings as often as you can afford to. A complimentary consultation may end up bringing you a substantial amount of business in the future.
- Suggest a drawing for a complimentary Staging consultation as part of a special event or holiday party at a real estate agency.

- Team up with a real estate agent or broker to help produce an agency newsletter.
- Send your own newsletter regularly to every agent in town.
- Send postcards to agents regularly, to keep your name in front of them.
- Offer to work with a broker to feature a Staged Home of the Month in local newspaper ads. If you are an ASP Stager, use the designation in the advertisement as well as the registered trademark symbol for the word "Stage."
- Be creative. Ideas are unlimited when you give your imagination free rein!

REFERRALS

Referrals are the lifeblood of any Stager. When you establish a few good relationships with real estate agents, expect them to refer you for Staging projects. Once you demonstrate your talent and skills as a Stager, they will be pleased and excited by the results. Be sure to ask them to refer you to others.

I like to keep agents in the loop about projects I'm working on and give them progress reports. Once a house has been Staged, I often invite the listing agent over for a small reception—perhaps a gathering for some crackers and cheese hosted by the homeowners, my Staging team, and me. Always check with the homeowners first, and if they agree, suggest that the listing agent invite a few coworkers and perhaps some clients to the Staged house. Ask the homeowners to invite neighbors and friends, too. Showing off your Staging work like this can pay dividends. People are impressed by the results and because seeing is believing, lingering doubts about the value of Staging will disappear. Another plus is that this could very well lead to more Staging projects.

All these strategies are effective ways to get your work noticed, but do not expect brokers to automatically refer clients to you. You have to work hard to keep your name and successes in their minds, but if you market yourself well, you will stay in the collective consciousness of the real estate community. And that, my dear Stager, is crucial.

Make sure you refer business to the real estate community whenever possible. When acquaintances or friends want to list their houses for sale, recommend an agent with whom you have worked. Ask the sellers to mention your name when they call the agent. Go to StagedHomes.com to find a trained ASP real estate agent to list the house.

SPECIAL CHALLENGES

Are you ever going to hear the word *no*? As my dad used to say, "You betcha!" I believe that every *no* is actually a step closer to *yes*. But you might as well get the negatives out of the way. Family members, friends, and colleagues may think it's helpful to tell you that you will never make money doing "this Staging thing." Get a real job, they'll advise. No one has heard the word *no* in reference to Home Staging as often as I have. For years, just about any time I suggested that sellers stage their house, I was told no. Sellers were not familiar with the concept of Staging and were wary of it. When I toured the country for 13 years speaking to more than a million real estate professionals about Home Staging, people began to catch on. Nevertheless, there are still millions of people who do not know what Home Staging is, and it's our job to educate them, one real estate agent or homeowner at a time.

When you feel discouraged, remember how far the profession has come since I started Staging in 1974. Persistence demonstrates how dedicated you are and how much you believe in what you are doing. While I say, "Never to take no for an answer," you will at times be frustrated by someone who is not interested in your message. This will likely be the case with certain real estate agents, and a few may simply be lost causes; however, many others will be willing and ready to work with you, and they are just waiting for you to appear. Never give up on the lost causes, either. I have discovered that most can eventually be won over.

Don't overwhelm any one agent with too many postcards, e-mails, or phone calls. Once you make the initial contact and don't get a positive response, give the agent some time. But never give up completely. Send the agent your newsletter and a note once in a while, as well as a card during the holidays. After a couple months have passed, call the agent again. He or she may have learned more about Staging in the interim and might be more receptive this time. I have occasionally dealt with initially reluctant agents who suddenly had Staging "emergencies" and insisted I was the only person who could help them salvage the listing. It happens. So never give up on any possibility. I have been doing this for 35 years, and I've witnessed similar situations time and again.

When agents tell you that they already work with a Stager, follow the advice in Chapter 7. Smile broadly and say something like this: "That's just great! I am so excited that you appreciate the value of Staging. Please keep my business card. And here is a certificate for a complimentary Home Staging consultation with me whenever you want to use it. When you find yourself in a bind, I hope you will call me!" Or you might try another pitch that has worked for me: "Sooner or later you are going to need me, and I will be ready to go work with you whenever you call." Both of these approaches have resulted in Staging projects and rewarding relationships with real estate agents. (Whatever you do, don't slink away, with a meek, "Thanks anyhow. I am sorry to have bothered you . . .") When one of these agents finally calls, never say, "I told you so!" Thank the agent and offer the best service you can.

You will also inevitably encounter real estate agents who claim they know all there is to know about Staging—and that they don't need your services. Never argue with these agents, but employ the tactic described previously. Smile warmly and offer your business card and a certificate for a complimentary service. Believe me, when their listings do not sell, you will be the first person they call.

Many real estate agents think they know how to Stage, believing it's all about a vase of fresh flowers and opening the drapes. If you have the opportunity to show them my DVD *How to Stage Your Home to Sell for Top Dollar!* they will immediately see that they do not have the time, much less the skill, to Stage their listings. Once real estate brokers see how we Stage homes, they usually realize that selling and Staging are not the same thing. They then recognize that they need us to Stage their listings to sell. Remember, real estate agents list and sell houses. When they are good at their job, they do not have the time to Stage their properties.

So my best advice to you as a Stager is to keep at it. Work to establish connections with as many agents as possible, and be both patient and persistent. Keep your name in front of every real estate professional you know of, work hard on the projects you have, and keep your Career Book up to date. As your reputation grows, the work will come.

It's one of life's inevitabilities that when the work comes, it will come in bunches. Mary DeBella, an ASPM Stager, e-mailed me over the course of several months, bemoaning the lack of work. I replied, "Stick with it. Plant one seed after the other and sooner or later they will sprout!" And sprout they did. I will never forget the day when Mary's e-mail read: "Oh, my gosh, I just booked six Stagings today! Six of them!" The work flow hasn't stopped for Mary, and it won't for you. Today, she is the number one stager in Portland, Oregon.

Now it is your turn. Dream the dream and never give up. Persist! Persist! Persist! The best is yet to come. I am thrilled that I stuck with it all this time. There has not been a single day in all those 35 years when I doubted the magic and the power that are Home Staging. Staging is to houses what merchandising is to stores, and what detailing is to cars. It's the extra something special that sells houses, the creative energy that benefits everyone who comes into contact with it. I thank God for the gift of this concept.

The next chapter goes beyond the concept and plunges into the action of Home Staging.

CHAPTER 9

LIGHTS, CAMERA, ACTION! ACTUAL STAGING

Buyers only know what they see, not the way it's going to be.
—BARB SCHWARZ

Finally! It's time to let your new business take you where you want to be: Staging a house. You have named your business, secured the necessary licenses, purchased sufficient insurance, and set up a business telephone line and e-mail address. You have determined how you will charge, and you have creative ideas for marketing yourself.

You should be good to go!

BARB'S STAGING GUIDELINES

In Chapter 5, you read about the basics of Home Staging. By now, you should understand that the purpose of Staging is to turn a house or condominium into a product that can be marketed for sale. Your job as a Stager is to assess what needs to be done in any given home so that the greatest number of potential buyers will be able to envision living in the space.

To help you achieve success, I have devised a number of guidelines. Thus, the information in this chapter constitutes a road map for your journey toward successful Staging. As mentioned in Chapter 5, the Three C's of Staging are *clean, clutter free,* and *color.* Let's tackle these first.

- *Clean:* This means that the house should be what I call Q-tip clean. Buyers should be able to run their fingers along the top of a door frame or on a bathroom counter and come away without a smudge. Walls should be scrubbed to remove all scuff marks, and carpets and drapes need to be cleaned. If the house smells from pets or tobacco, use products that eliminate or minimize the odor. Figures 9.1 and 9.2 show before and after views of a bedroom that was cleaned and Staged.

- *Clutter free:* Most of us don't see our own clutter. It's your job as a Stager to zero in on it and explain to homeowners how to get rid of it. Talk to the homeowners before anyone attacks the clutter and ask them to help eliminate it. Have them pack up their doll or model ship collections. They need to remove the knickknacks that cover the end tables, and clear out at least a third of the books on overstuffed shelves. Remove the family photos lining the walls and stairways. Recycle the piles of magazines. Pack up the dozens of stuffed animals and put away all but the nicest of the throw pillows. Get rid of outdated telephone books, and ask the homeowners to sort through the stacks of paper on the kitchen counters and desk. Pull the mismatched pots and pans out of the cupboards and return only those that are the best looking and most useful. Do the same for the coat closet and mudroom bins jammed

Figure 9.1 **Before ASP Staging**

Figure 9.2 **After ASP Staging**

Figure 9.3 **Before ASP Staging**

Figure 9.4 **After ASP Staging**

Figure 9.5 **Before ASP Staging**

Figure 9.6 **After ASP Staging**

full of boots, ice skates, and old scarves and mittens. Figures 9.3 and 9.4 show a living room that was decluttered during Staging.

- *Color:* The object of Staging is to make every room look clean and fresh. Your first thought might be to paint, but I have found that a good scrubbing often saves the homeowners money. Some cleaning products are so effective that there may be no reason to repaint rooms. For instance, one of my favorites, Krud Kutter, takes most scuff marks off walls and woodwork. For white walls or woodwork, a little dab of Liquid Paper or Wite-Out can sometimes fill in cracks. Of course, sometimes a room simply needs a fresh coat of paint. If the paint job is very old, flaking off, and beyond cleaning, suggest repainting. If the color is extreme, suggest repainting—for example, a teenager's room that is painted black or dark purple (I have seen these colors in teenagers' rooms more often than you might imagine), a bathroom painted lipstick pink, or a kitchen painted pea green. Use your good sense when discussing color with the homeowners. We are Stagers, not decorators, and our job is to neutralize the excessive. Remind homeowners that dark colors make rooms appear small, while neutral colors make them seem larger. This resonates with sellers and agents, as we are all about helping to sell the space. The before and after views of the little girl's room in Figures 9.5 and 9.6 are a case in point.

BARB'S TOP 15 STAGING GUIDELINES

Beyond the Three C's, I recommend some more specific guidelines for executing a successful Staging. The first one is "Less is more," and I cannot sufficiently emphasize how critical this is. When in doubt, repeat this to yourself. When you stand in the doorway of a room you have Staged but find that it is not quite what you are aiming for, you can usually spot one area you can declutter even further. Presto! Now you have Staging perfection.

Here are my top 15 Staging guidelines:

1. Less is more.
2. Three is the magic number for Staging: three items on a table, three pieces of furniture in a vignette, and three framed pictures on a wall.
3. Arrange groupings of items that are high, medium, and low in relation to each other. For example, on a table you might place a lamp (high), a vase (medium), and a book (low). Position them in a rough triangle, which is the primary configuration to use when arranging furniture and accessories. With the principle of high, medium, and low, this will help you Stage in all sorts of situations. I rely on the power of three.
4. Give all items breathing room. Don't crowd things on shelves, countertops, dressers, or tables. Ditto for furniture.
5. Avoid the *Titanic* principle. When the ocean liner sank, it listed to one side. Don't position furniture or items in the room so that they weigh down one side of it. Large, heavy furniture should be balanced with smaller, lighter objects throughout a room.
6. Let the light in. Remove heavy drapery; open shades; wash the windows. Check that electric lights are working and no bulbs are blown.
7. Use nature to Stage by bringing the outside inside. Cut greenery from the yard and use it creatively inside the house in each room. The color green signifies abundance, and the beauty this brings to a room can make a big difference. Add a touch of green to every room and let it do its magic.
8. Rely on your creativity to solve problems. Your own ingenuity usually is sufficient, but if you are stumped or in need of some inspiration, go to StagedHomes.com for fresh

ideas. Keep handy my best-selling book *Home Staging: The Winning Way to Sell Your House for More Money,* which is packed with Staging ideas.

9. Reduce the amount of furniture in any room, which creates more space. Trust me, you will sense when there is too much furniture in a room. Removing some furniture from one room and using it elsewhere in the house can often resolve the whole problematic situation.

10. Invent new uses for items. I have used fishing rods as curtain rods, sheets as window valances, drapes as bedspreads, and bedspreads as tablecloths. Let your imagination run free.

11. Eliminate the clutter. (Remember the Three C's of Staging!) As I always say, "Clutter eats equity."

12. Use color for accent pieces and accessories, such as throw pillows, a scarf artfully draped over a table or lamp, or a glass bowl filled with colored glass beads, but in general, keep strong colors off the walls. There are exceptions to everything, but my experience indicates that walls painted in dominant colors keep houses from selling. When you Stage, color should be used only as an accent.

13. Hang pictures at the average woman's eye level.

14. If a picture is too high, lower it or hang another picture or decorative piece below it to make a unit.

15. Paint is a small investment that garners the highest rate of return. I like to paint the back and sides of bookcases, which creates drama and automatically adds depth to the whole room.

I can't say it enough: Staging works! To reaffirm that, Mariagrace Welsh, an ASP Stager in New Jersey, tells this story: "I met a homeowner who was very frustrated because her condominium had been on the market [for months] with no offers. She had taken a price reduction and still nothing. A friend had mentioned Staging but she had no idea what it meant. When I met with her and explained the benefits and affordability of Staging her one-bedroom condo she decided to give it a try. We Staged the property and 12 days later it was under contract. The homeowner and the real estate agent were ecstatic." Mariagrace adds, "The amazing thing is that there were other condos in the complex for sale in the same price range but buyers chose hers. Staged homes don't have a problem getting offers, even when the market is slow."

BARB'S 12 STEPS FOR STAGING A ROOM IN AN OCCUPIED HOUSE

The 15 guidelines are important, and they will stand you in good stead when you Stage. Even after you have become a seasoned Stager, read them over every so often. You will be surprised how quickly they refocus you on the task at hand. Here are the 12 steps for Staging a room. Like the 15 guidelines, tailor them to the contracted project.

1. Stand in the doorway of the room to get a feel for it. Determine the purpose of the room (sleep, study, home office, relaxation, hobbies, and so on).
2. Select the Staging point of the room. If it's a dining room, this would be the table; a bedroom, the bed; a living room, the sofas or the fireplace; a bathroom, the tub or the vanity. When there is a view, it takes precedence over everything else. Make the most of it.
3. Make a plan for Staging the room. You can do this in your head, but I find it useful to write notes. First impressions are extremely valuable and, although the plan inevitably will change, starting without one will have you running in circles. Plan your Staging strategy, but remain open to change.
4. Deaccessorize. I have used this word so much that it's

entered the vocabulary of every ASP Home Stager. This is an important part of Home Staging. Take the knickknacks off the tables, books from the shelves, pictures from the wall, and pillows off the furniture. Deaccessorize the whole room.

5. Divide the accessories in the room into two piles: one to keep, the other to use in other rooms or pack up. It's a good idea to ask the homeowners to go through the house beforehand to remove valuables and breakables, and to discard the junk. I love 1-800-Got Junk, a company that hauls away anything except chemicals—and they do it with class. They arrive dressed in uniforms, and their trucks are clean. (When I met the owner of the company, he told me that his mother was an ASP Stager, which thrilled me.)

6. Pack what you don't use in boxes. Use lots of packing tissue, bubble wrap, or both, and be extremely careful. The way you pack is crucial because you are responsible for any breakage. This is why I always ask the homeowners to remove their breakable valuables. Clearly mark the boxes to indicate the specific room in which they belong. I note what is inside the box, too ("children's toys from blue bedroom"; "vases, framed photos, and sports trophies from family room"). The sellers will appreciate it. Always keep duplicate lists, for you and the seller, of the major items you pack.

7. Look at the furniture with fresh eyes. You do not have to move every piece out of the room. Decide what will work and what should go. Many homeowners have too much furniture in their rooms; your job is to remove everything that is not necessary.

8. Move the furniture you don't want out of the room. Check the other rooms first, to see whether these pieces would work elsewhere. Pack them up to store in the garage or use a PODS storage container. Never move a piece of furniture without looking beneath it and on top of it. I have found guns, dirty diapers, jewelry, artwork, books, cameras, and far more that

I would prefer not to mention here. You don't want a book to hit you in the face or a gun to misfire! Nor would you want to accidentally stand on a framed picture and crack the glass. If you find anything of value or that is dangerous, leave it where it is and call the real estate agent. The homeowners may have forgotten about it when they gathered up their valuables, but you don't want to be responsible for it. Postpone Staging the room until the owner removes it.

9. Arrange the remaining furniture so that it looks best from the doorway of the room. This is where buyers will first view the room, so it's vital to make a good impression from this vantage point. Stage the room to enhance flow and create a sense of space, so that potential buyers feel there is enough room for their own furniture. The homeowners are selling space, and it's our job as Stagers to reveal that space. Staging sets the scene so that the right buyer will say, "This is where I want to live."

10. Reaccessorize the room with items from other rooms in the house or from your inventory. Keep them simple, classy, and clean looking. When you Stage an occupied house, you very often do not have to bring in anything from elsewhere. Frequently, the homeowners will have everything you need.

11. Balance soft and hard surfaces in the room. This means mixing stuffed furniture with what I call stick furniture: An upholstered sofa is soft, while a straight-backed chair is stick furniture. Upholstery should extend to the floor on at least one piece of furniture in the room. For example, an upholstered sofa and two wingback chairs with exposed legs is ideal. Or if the bedspread reaches the floor, put a tall-boy chest in the bedroom, too.

12. Last but not least, return to the doorway and take another look. Fine-tune the Staging. Make sure pictures are straight, cords are out of sight, curtains are even, and so forth.

When you Stage a vacant home, follow the same procedure but use your own inventory along with rented furniture, if necessary. These 12 steps are equally effective, whether the house is occupied or vacant. Staging is Staging, and if you follow these guidelines and procedures, you will be satisfied with the results—and so will your clients! Build your inventory or rent what you need—the next section explains how to do this.

BUY OR RENT WHAT YOU NEED

During the coming months and years, you will Stage one house after another, and in the process, you will acquire an inventory of Staging supplies. Take your time building this inventory. Not only does this help control cash flow, but it makes sense to assemble what you need deliberately and with a good deal of care. To start, you might take items from your own house, such as vases, plates, and tablecloths, but you soon will discover that it's preferable to stock up on these and other items expressly for your business.

Like most people, I love to shop. Put me in a store, and I am happy as can be. Let's face it, if you like to Stage properties, you probably enjoy selecting things that you think will help the house sell when you Stage it. When you are a Stager, your eye is always scanning for items that might work in any given house. What about those towels? That framed landscape painting? Those oversized urns? The nest of wicker tables? Those colorful pillows or the assortment of pillar candles? It's good practice to start looking at nearly everything through the eyes of a Stager.

Stores such as Target, Linens-N-Things, Pier 1, and Wal-Mart, are gold mines for Stagers. They offer housewares for the kitchen, bathroom, bedroom, and living areas, as well as furnishings suitable for the patio and front porch, and they are usually very reasonably priced. Also terrific are stores such as Home Depot for inexpensive garden supplies and flowers, hardware, tools, and any number of fixtures for the home. Office supply outlets and craft supply stores are great places for tape, scissors, ribbon, raffia (my personal favorite), and markers.

A top-notch Stager is a savvy shopper. Unless you can tell me, for example, the price range of the pillows sold at Target and how they compare to those sold at Wal-Mart—and exactly where they are in the store nearest you—you do not know as much as you should. This is important because you never know when a call might come for a Staging project. You might need to locate accessories quickly, and it's not fair to you or your client if you spend hours driving from one store to the next, and then even more time in the stores searching for stock items. If you love Staging as much as I do—and if you are reading this book, I suspect you do—then developing this skill will be more fun than tiresome.

In Chapter 4 I suggested that you earmark a percentage of your monthly income for inventory. This could be 2 percent, 5 percent, or 10 percent, and the amount is bound to fluctuate as your business grows and as you build your inventory. You will always need basic supplies, such as tape, packing materials, ribbon, and cleaning supplies. Anyone who has taken an ASP Staging course has heard me teasingly lament how "that raffia investment really adds up," but the truth is that Stagers do not incur tremendous expenses. You should be paid for your creative talent, not for the stuff you cart into clients' houses.

Some supplies will need frequent replenishing, others will keep for years, while still others you will want to recycle every so often. I like to sell these recyclables at fund-raising tag sales organized by a worthwhile charity in my hometown, or I give them to new ASP Stagers who come on board and help me with projects. Because they are just starting out, these Stagers are happy to take some of my inventory as payment for their services, and I am happy to give them pieces that still have a lot of life in them but which I am replacing with newer things for one reason or another.

Check with your accountant, but usually items that you purchase exclusively for your Staging business are tax deductible. I cannot say this categorically, so I urge you to double-check with your financial advisor.

When I Stage an occupied house, I strive not to rent many items, preferring to rely on what the client has in the house instead. But when a property is vacant or there is simply no other option, renting is fantastic. Clever Stagers know how to mix and match what clients have with what is in their own inventory and then fill any gaps with rentals.

When you use products from your inventory, charge the home-owners a monthly rental fee. I use the same rule of thumb the furniture rental companies use, which is to charge 20 percent of the cost of the item. For example, if you set a table with chargers, plates, bowls, and stemware that you paid $75 for, charge a monthly fee of $15. If you accent the homeowners' sofa with three brightly colored accent pillows that you picked up at a yard sale for a dollar apiece, it is not practical to charge a monthly rental rate of 60 cents. Attach a fixed dollar amount, such as $5, or group the pillows with other linens and charge one overall rate.

You might prefer to do what a lot of ASP Stagers do and set inventory rental fees based on the room that is being Staged. For example, you might charge from $250 to $400 a month for a living room, and perhaps a little less for a bathroom. Add up what you put in the room and then figure out a fair price for the rentals. The rentals might include artwork, rugs, small pieces of furniture, and perhaps a ficus tree. You own these things, so it's your right to charge what you think you need. You also should take into consideration that when they are being used in one Staged home, they are not available for use in another house, so the rental fee should compensate you for this as well.

When you rent items to a client, charge a month in advance to cover your costs and help control cash flow. Chapter 6 explains how to set up a merchant account so that homeowners can pay you with a bank or debit card. This keeps everything simple and business-like, and protects you from accepting bad checks.

HOW TO RENT FURNITURE

I always say that if I can't lift it, I don't buy it. This is where the rental companies come in handy. You can rent just about anything, from sofas and dining sets to lamps, television sets, carpets, and matching dinner service for eight. I have a secret: My Chicago condominium is furnished entirely with rentals from Brook Furniture Rental, and I couldn't be happier. I figure that when I get tired of that particular style, I will just rent a different one!

Be thankful for furniture rental companies. Without them, you might have to invest in tens of thousands of dollars worth of furniture to run a successful Staging business, not to mention a warehouse to store it . . .

If the house you are Staging is lived in, chances are good that you can use the furniture that is already in it to Stage it. As you learn when you take the three-day ASP Staging course, a good piece of furniture can become the centerpiece or a lively accent for a room. It might be hiding in an upstairs bedroom, but when moved to the living room or great room, it pops.

However, furniture that is worn, torn, chipped, or frankly outlandish generally has no place in a Staged home. This furniture needs to go into storage, unless the sellers decide to get rid of it. If the home has too many of these pieces, you might find it necessary to fill out a room or two with rented furniture. I have Staged occupied homes that had three or four empty rooms. What did I do? I moved furniture from other rooms and then rented what I needed.

Work with large rental companies, such as Brook Furniture Rental and CORT Furniture Rental. These companies have extensive inventories, reliable delivery service, and track records you can depend on. They keep their stock in tip-top shape and are able to buy new pieces all the time. In fact, Brook is dedicated to turning over its inventory every quarter, a fact that I find amazing and is wonderful for Stagers.

In its literature, Brook Furniture Rental makes this statement:

"Homes that were Staged before listing sold in less than 1.5 months. Homes listed without Staging were on the market an average of 4.5 months before selling." Very recently, the company relayed a set of revealing statistics to me about some vacant houses in the Chicago area that were not selling. Professional ASP Stagers were called in and with the help of furniture rentals from Brook, worked their wonders as you can quickly see from the stats.

A house in Chicago's northern suburbs, listed for $1,850,000, had been on the market for one year and four months. Once Staged, it sold in 120 days. Another house in the northern suburbs sold for the listing price of $740,000 in *one* day after being Staged; it had been on the market for nine months. In the western suburbs, a house listed for $1.2 million sold in 60 days after Staging. Before Staging, it had sat vacant and unsold for three months. Finally, a million-dollar property in Chicago sat on the market for two years before it was Staged. What happened? It sold in 30 days.

As explained in Chapter 6, you should not pick up the tab for the rental company. The seller pays for the rental; you don't. You can recommend the company, select the pieces that will work in the home, and be there when they are delivered, but you should not front the money. This is the responsibility of the homeowners, which you should make clear when you discuss the investment they will make in Staging the property. Do this even if you don't expect to rent a single thing. You never know.

HOW TO STAGE A VACANT HOUSE

Whether it's a builder house in a development or a house recently vacated by a family forced to move because of a job transfer, vacant houses need to be Staged. They offer their own creative challenge. And I love it!

When a house is empty, it can be much easier to Stage because you start with a blank canvas, an empty page, a dark theater, and an empty set. Conversely, there is nothing there to work with and you, the Stager, have to bring large as well as small pieces onto the property. Less is more, but when you start with nothing, you need a little more!

Walk through the house and talk with the real estate agent. Remember, the whole property needs to be Staged whether it is lived in or vacant. This means the interior of the house and the outside areas, too. When an agent or seller suggests I Stage a few rooms only—say, the living room, dining room, and master bedroom—I counter by asking if they are planning to sell the rest of the rooms. I pause and then add, "The only rooms that will sell are the Staged ones. If you don't Stage them all, the buyer will say the house doesn't work, that it's too small or too big, or it doesn't feel like home." If this happens, I remind them that they have lost that buyer. You don't get second chances in real estate because you have only one opportunity to make a first impression. If the other rooms are not Staged and seem crowded or cold and uninviting, buyers will reject the whole house. Staging part of a house is never a good idea because you cannot sell half a house.

If the clients are concerned about budget, work with them to make it viable. Use fewer pieces in more rooms, for example. Dig deep into your creative bag of tricks and look at this as an opportunity to grow. Rely on the rule of three and Stage small vignettes throughout the house, using just a few large pieces. Pull them from the walls and corners to accentuate the dimensions of the room. It's not hard to warm up a room without trucking in a lot of furniture and accessories. For an example of an empty home that was Staged, see Figures 9.7 and 9.8.

I look at the world differently than most people, and you, as a Home Stager, must do the same. Everywhere I go, I look for potential Staging items, accessories, furniture, props, and fun things, too. I keep an eye out for items that are meant for another purpose but in which I see potential for Staging. Keep your antennae up; you never know what you will find. I collect items from tag sales, estate

Figure 9.7 **Before ASP Staging**

Figure 9.8 **After ASP Staging**

sales, store closeouts, and discount sales and from relatives and friends who are tired of their old things and want to try something new. As long as it is safe, legal, moral, and accessible, I grab it!

When you Stage a vacant house, you may first think of having the seller rent furniture, and surely doing so would solve some of the immediate problems. But you need to look to your inventory, too. You will find any number of useful things that can Stage a room successfully before you need to rent furniture.

I heard from Darla Rowley, ASP, IAHSP, about an empty condominium she was hired to Stage in a community with six units left to sell. It was the "problem unit" she said because of the tile entry, Berber carpet, and harsh black appliances. She and her team integrated black accents into the kitchen area with bar stools and a black café set. They added a $30 mantle and a $70 rug for a "punch of color to the entry and to soften the coldness of the tile." She said that they created an "outdoor vignette on the deck, the [only pieces] we rented to the builder and the only things the buyers wanted included in the sale." The condo was the first of the final six to sell.

Once the house is Staged, plan to check on it every week or 10 days. When buyers and agents walk through it, they move things around. They might have moved a chair from one room to another when they made a cell phone call. Maybe they moved the throw pillows from the sofa to a chair. You never know, and it's important to maintain the integrity of your creation.

YOUR STAGING INVENTORY

Your Staging inventory is an important business asset, and I suggest that you keep yours under control. Acquire what you need, discard what you don't use, and never stock up on unnecessary items.

I keep an inventory of furniture and accessories for Staging. It's all stored neatly, cataloged, and organized so that I can find whatever

I need easily and efficiently. These are the tools of our trade. Treat them with respect. Clean and repair them when you de-Stage properties. Throw out anything that is past its prime or set it aside for a tag sale or to give to a new Stager. Mark everything that you keep with your name. I print my own labels that say: "This item belongs to Barb Schwarz," and I add my telephone number. I carry the labels in my truck, my car, my ASP apron, and my custom-designed ASP Staging caddy. If I stop by one of my Stagings and discover that a label has fallen off an item, I can replace it on the spot.

Your inventory might resemble mine, although we may not include exactly the same items. Remember that I have built my inventory over the years, and to this day I keep adding to it. Here is a list of some of the most important items to keep in your inventory:

- King-size flat white, beige, or cream-colored sheets. I put these over large plastic patio tables in the kitchen or dining room. The tables, which measure 36 to 48 inches across, are easy to find in hardware stores. They are useful for creating a draped look that I like in a lot of houses and gardens. I also use the sheets for bedding, regardless of the size of bed; you can tuck in the king-size sheets. I use them for drapes by knotting them together and then swagging them over curtain rods. You cannot have too many crisp, clean sheets in your inventory.
- Tapestries, scarves, sarongs, and throws to overlay the sheets on tables. I sometimes glue tassels along the edge of certain fabrics or tapestries to dress them up a little. These are great on tables and can be used to partially cover windows, too.
- Inexpensive chairs and covers. I buy the covers from catalogs or home stores. They give rounded plastic chairs or simple wooden chairs a clean, neat appearance.
- Wicker furniture. All sizes and colors work, and wicker is light and easy to move from room to room. Wicker is espe-

cially effective in children's rooms, sunrooms, and kitchens. I use expensive-looking dark wicker in the family rooms of large, high-priced homes. Go with your feelings.

- Afghans and quilts of all sizes. These can be used for window coverings and tablecloths, and can even be folded into square pillow shapes, which I tie with ribbon or my famous "hairy rope" (rough twine). Raffia works well, too.

- Decorative pillows for beds, sofas, and chairs in all sizes and colors.

- Inflatable camp beds and "beds in a bag." The camp beds come with bed frames and once you make them with linens, it's hard to tell that they are not more permanent beds. You can purchase these online or at stores such as Wal-Mart in the camping department. I suggest twin and queen-size beds. You can push two twins together for a king-size bed. I put warning signs on them that say: "Please do not sit on bed."

- Several sets of towels. I favor black towels because they add drama while maintaining a sleek look, and they don't show dirt. For children's bathrooms, I prefer towels in bright solid colors.

- Area rugs. Even large ones don't cost too much at discount, high-volume stores. Go for the look rather than the price, and arrange them to get the optimum effect. Don't put furniture directly on top of the rugs, and keep them visible.

- Small, high-quality, and upscale rugs for the bathrooms. I also use rugs in the bathrooms that would normally belong in other rooms. Make sure you have a nonskid pad or backing on the rugs. (I stay away from the fuzzy look in bathrooms. Rather than dressing up the rooms, they make bathrooms look cheap.)

- Small wooden chairs and tables to place next to them. These can be used throughout the house.

- Standing lamps. These provide light, don't require a table, and can fit just about anywhere in the house.

- Wall art. Discount stores sell it quite cheaply. Go for large pictures or groups of three small ones that work well together. Sometimes the frames are the best part—I have been known to buy a cheap picture just for the frame.
- Children's table and chairs. These are marvelous when you Stage a child's bedroom. They are not expensive, and I suggest you buy both wooden ones and colorful plastic tables and chairs. I also like the cute patio sets you can find at large supermarkets.
- Toys and stuffed animals. Go for a few big stuffed animals rather than a bunch of small ones. I use stuffed animals in children's rooms, but I also put them in unexpected places like a bathroom or on a curtain rod.
- Dishes, chargers, water glasses and stemware, napkins, napkin rings, and place mats. Have several sets in several colors. The more choices you have, the more fun you will have. Never use cutlery when you Stage. It could double as a weapon and therefore is not considered safe. When you creatively Stage a kitchen or dining room table with a great piece of fabric, oversized chargers, dishes, stemware, and a great centerpiece, no one will miss the silverware.
- Ironwork, such as lanterns, bowls, baskets, mirrors, and candlesticks.
- Baskets of all sizes.
- Silk plants, flowers, and vines. Go for quality when you see it. Shop around, shop around, and shop around!
- Dried flowers. These damage easily so be careful about the ones you purchase and how you store them.
- Fake ficus trees, both large and small. These can be costly, so look for them at garage sales or buy them when stores like Wal-Mart have sales.
- Plant stands made of wire, wicker, metal, or wood. These provide good focal points in hallways, entries, and large rooms. I love plant stands and have numerous ones in all

colors and styles. They look classy with nothing more than a bundle of clipped grasses and twigs, or I top them with a French milk can. Beautiful!

- Up-to-date decorating magazines, such as *Architectural Digest* and *Dwell*. I use these as accent pieces to warm up the house. Make sure the colors that dominate the cover work with the Staging theme. Be picky.
- Ribbons, grass ropes, twine, raffia. These are useful to tie around rolled towels, to catch curtains, and to tie around small bouquets. I love raffia, whether it's natural or colored. I buy it by the yard. I always tell the ASP Stagers I train that raffia is to women as duct tape is to men (just writing it down makes me laugh!).
- Radios for every floor in the house. Music should play on all levels of the house and all radios should be tuned to the same easy-listening station.

Beyond the inventory of Staging items, every Stager needs supplies. While many of these may seem obvious, if you happen to overlook any, you will miss them when you are working on a Staging project.

Keep your supplies organized and fresh. I designed a wheeled caddy to carry my supplies, which is available to ASP Stagers on our web site, StagedHomes.com. The caddy has a long handle, similar to the carry-on luggage we all use in airports, and inside it has compartments for the numerous tools every Stager needs.

When I think of the myriad things that fall into the supplies category, the list seems endless. Here is as complete a list as I can make. I am sure you will have your own ideas of things to add.

- Electric drill and screwdriver.
- Assorted manual screwdrivers.
- Hammer.
- Small nails, brads, and screws.

- Level.
- Pliers.
- Measuring tape.
- Electrical tape.
- Masking tape, transparent tape, and packing tape.
- Craft and wood glues.
- Scissors.
- Wite-Out.
- Rubber bands.
- Packing tissue.
- Bubble wrap.
- Packing boxes (you probably will want these delivered to the house; order them through www.aspboxes.com).
- Picture hangers, wire, and hooks.
- Rubber gloves.
- Lightbulbs.
- Timers for lights (especially important for vacant houses).
- Plug-in cell phone charger (this is very important; you do not want to work alone without a phone).
- Car charger for the cell phone.
- Small step stool.
- Furniture lifter (these are available at StagedHomes.com; they jack up furniture effortlessly).
- Moving pads (these are also available at StagedHomes.com; they slide under the furniture so you can move it easily).
- Steamer (useful for drapery and linens).
- Toilet paper.
- Garbage bags.
- Twine.
- Rope (clothesline works, too).
- Ribbon.
- Raffia.
- Markers.

- Staging labels for marking items as yours.
- Hinged clips. These work for thick stacks of paper when paper clips won't do. They come in assorted colors.
- Paper clips.
- Outdoor clippers for shrubbery.

WORKING WITH VENDORS

When you Stage a property, you do not work in a vacuum. You rely on a number of vendors, such as PODS (which stands for "portable on-demand storage"), Pier 1, Linens-N-Things, 1-800-GOT-JUNK, Sherwin Williams paint, and furniture rental companies such as Brook Furniture Rental.

I have established relationships with these companies so that you, as an ASP Stager, can get discounts and pass them on to your clients (or not). Go to StagedHomes.com for the details on what's available to ASP Stagers.

This is one of those ideas that makes good sense. We are in the business of taking the home out of the house so that it becomes a marketable product, and to do so we need the help of any number of vendors.

Work with the vendors that support Home Staging. You might want to approach some local businesses to work out cooperative deals with them. These could be garden nurseries, hardware stores, and houseware suppliers.

Once you start Staging, you get bitten by the bug. It's creative and fun, and it can also be lucrative. What could be better? I love to Stage, and my enthusiasm has proven to be contagious. You will be successful, but you must be persistent. Don't give up! I am excited for everyone who starts a new endeavor that involves Staging. I am sure by now you are eager to start Staging. In the next chapter, I will share my hopes for and assessment of the future of Home Staging.

CHAPTER 10

THE FUTURE OF HOME STAGING

Be the change you want to see in the world.
—BARB SCHWARZ

During the many years I have sold real estate, I have learned one true thing: People do not buy a home until they can envision themselves living in it.

I don't care what the circumstances are. This truth does not change. No buyers will put down good money if they cannot see their family or themselves living in a particular space.

This holds true, too, for commercial properties. While the tenant or business customer does not plan to live on the premises, he or she must be able to imagine doing business and making money there.

To state the obvious, this is where Staging plays a starring role, and I predict that this role will only grow in coming years.

A BRIEF HISTORY OF SELLING

Before we look to the future, let's take a quick look back to how real estate has traditionally been sold. When they decide to sell, sellers call a real estate agent. This means they put their most valuable asset in the hands of a local agent who, they hope, knows the market and has a proven track record of moving properties.

Sellers rely on the real estate pro to sell their house with a marketing plan that includes ads in newspapers and on web sites, a brokers' open house to expose the house to as many agents as possible, and a public open house to attract buyers off the street. I know how this works, and as a real estate broker, I assure you it's a proven system. Every year, millions and millions of dollars of real estate are sold following this tried-and-true formula.

Because I believe in the real estate industry, I positioned Home Staging firmly in it. But as much as I believe in real estate, I believe even more in the value of Home Staging. It is the single most important factor when it comes to selling a house—bar none. I even developed a recipe to define the elements that help a sale.

Barb's Recipe for a Sale

Location.
Condition.
Price.
Terms available.
State of the market.
Home Staging.

1. Mix all together when you want to sell a house. All the ingredients should be added, but the most important one is Home Staging.
2. Wait for a very short period of time and expect a sale for very good money.

Yield: 1 sold property.

When you make a chocolate cake, you need flour, eggs, butter, and chocolate. Anyone who eats the cake thinks only of the chocolate and does not consider that flour is the common ingredient in every cake, whether it's a chocolate cake, angel food cake, orange cake, buttermilk cake, or any other kind. Home Staging is the flour in my recipe. You can vary a few of the other ingredients, but to get a sale (the cake); you need Home Staging (the flour) every time.

Sellers hear this recipe, and they usually nod their heads in agreement when the real estate broker mentions location. You've heard the refrain: "Location, location, location!"

Yes, location is important and does affect price; however, Home Staging impacts price *regardless of location*. Market conditions affect all properties, too, so Staged homes have a competitive, financial edge. As I like to say, "Staging a home is a financially smart thing to do."

For these reasons, I predict that Home Staging will become a service that homeowners demand even before they list their houses. This shift in the paradigm is huge, with major implications for how the real estate industry will regard Staging in the future. When I first predicted this more than 10 years ago, most people did not take me seriously. Now, true believers are lining up to become Stagers and to have their properties Staged. Because I created the Home Staging industry and market, I imagine we have just begun to flourish, and I have a number of predictions for a glorious future.

BARB'S SIX TOP PREDICTIONS FOR THE FUTURE OF HOME STAGING

When I get "into the zone" and let my mind drift, I see no end to the opportunities Home Staging offers entrepreneurs who want to run their own businesses. My intuition has not let me down before, and I don't expect it to do so now; it tells me that for homeowners who want to get top dollar for their house or condominium in as short a time as possible, Staging is the answer now and will be even more effective in the future. For individuals who want to start businesses, the prospects provided by Home Staging are limitless. So here are my six predictions:

1. *Home Stagers, and ASP Home Stagers in particular, will play critical roles in setting the market.* As the public comes to understand the value of Staging, individual sellers will contact Home Stagers even before they call the real estate agent. Why? Because staging is a potent marketing tool. Already word of mouth is spreading about its significance and homeowners are starting to demand that their properties be Staged even before they are listed. This puts the ASP Stager in a position of control first and represents a momentous paradigm shift in the real estate industry. Now, the Stager will be able to pass on referrals to real estate agents rather than the other way around.

2. *Staging and real estate professionals will team up to sell houses.* Nowhere is this concept of teamwork more evident than in the ASP Staging courses that I offer. The first two days of the ASP course include both real estate agents and Home Stagers. The Home Stagers remain with me for the final day to learn much of what is contained between the covers of this book about running their own business. Having both professions together during the first two days is powerful. The agents learn how the Home Stagers work, and the Stagers learn how to work with the agents. From both perspectives, the goal is to best serve the seller. The real estate professionals learn about the value of Staging, how it works, and why it works. Together, Stagers and real estate professionals recognize the big-time value of collaboration. This makes a lot of sense.

   Productive real estate agents do not have time to Stage their listings—they have houses to list and sell. I have seen it happen time and again. Real estate agents take the ASP course and, although they admit being impressed by Staging, at the end of the day, they say, "Oh, well, I don't have time for this amount of work. Even if I did, I would rather suggest to sellers that they hire a trained Home Stager to do the work—or I might include Staging as part of my marketing plan." Bingo! When the skills of each complement the other, the results are spectacular. I predict that before long, real estate professionals will include Staging as part of their marketing plans, along with open houses and newspaper ads.

Recently, I spoke at the annual convention for the National Association of Realtors in New Orleans, Louisiana. I challenged those in attendance to provide the value-added service of Staging to their customers, or at least to commit to educating them about it. I recommended that the real estate agents team with ASP Stagers. I am pleased to say that the top agents are already heeding my call; many include the Stager's consultation fee in their marketing plan. It makes sense for agents to invest their own dollars in Staging to increase the possibility of a high return, and many are doing so. This will not be universal for some time. Most Home Stagers will continue to be paid by the homeowners rather than the real estate agents for the time being. But make no mistake about it: Home Staging is here to stay, and it is having a momentous impact on agents and the real estate industry in general.

3. *The way commissions and fees are structured will change.* Staging is a fee-based business and not commission based like real estate. When sellers list a house with a real estate agent, they negotiate a commission based on the listing price, which typically is 5, 6, or 7 percent. The sellers may also hire a Home Stager and pay a set amount for the creative service. Added to that may be furniture and accessory

rental fees and the cost of painting several rooms and completing other minor improvements to the property. (Because Staging has nothing to do with the condition of the house, more substantial improvements do no fall within its purview.)

I frequently hear about houses that sell immediately after they are Staged and before the real estate agents organize and implement open houses or local advertising campaigns. Understandably, the sellers might question the commissions the real estate agents are owed. Down the road, this will alter how agents charge for their services. It also underscores prediction number 2. The time will come when Staging is considered part of the real estate agent's marketing plan for nearly every listed property. Thus, I am confident that this prediction is right on the dime.

4. *The Home Staging industry will grow larger every year.* There's no stopping something as results-driven as Home Staging. Once sellers stage a house and it sells quickly and for the asking price (or more), they will want to Stage every subsequent real estate property they ever sell. Once real estate brokers see how much Staging helps sales, they will want to include it as part of every real estate transaction. As I say in predictions 2 and 3, I firmly believe that before too long, real estate agents will pay Stagers directly, rather than passing on the cost to homeowners. This will ensure that the houses get Staged properly and that the value of Staging is fully realized.

Home Stagers' earning potential will continue to grow. I urge the ASP Stagers I train to rely on their creativity and ingenuity when they Stage a property. With a good eye and fertile imagination, most Staging can be done with the furnishings already in an occupied home. This means that successful, productive Home Stagers can keep their overhead to a minimum and make very good money.

5. *ASP training leads the way.* To maximize your earning potential, I can't emphasize enough how important it is to become a certified ASP Stager. Every day ASP Stagers are called in to de-Stage and re-Stage properties that supposedly have been Staged by people who are neither trained nor qualified. Anyone can wake up and say, "I think I will become a Stager today," but as with any endeavor that is worth pursuing, it takes a lot more than simple desire. It takes time, commitment, training, and more training. ASP Stagers are trained in the standards, practices, policies, procedures, and skills necessary to serve both the public and the real estate community. Without this training, they do not qualify for the ASP designation. Since I first invented the concept of Home Staging, my goal has been to establish standards for the industry. It is my mission to keep the bar high and raise it whenever I can, and I dedicate every day of my life to doing just that.

6. *The real estate industry is here to stay—but it will include Stagers and Home Staging.* While Staging helps sell houses and condominiums quickly and for top dollar, it does not eliminate the need for real estate agents and brokers. As a broker who has sold more than 5,000 houses, I know this only too well. Real estate agents' jobs go far beyond securing buyers; they earn their fee or commission when they close the sale. And that's fundamental to ultimate success. Once a buyer makes an offer and it's accepted, there are any number of obstacles that can arise between then and the final sale. The building inspector might uncover structural problems with the property, the bank might refuse the buyers a mortgage, or the buyers might get cold feet. As a real estate agent, you occasionally might have to sell the same house two or three times. This means the career requirements for any real estate professional are demanding, and it explains why Staging is and will continue to be a collaborative business that is

only as successful as the real estate community in which it operates. I predict that those real estate agents who have ASP Stagers on their teams will be leaders in their market, regardless of the city or region in which they live.

INDUSTRY GROWTH BEYOND HOME STAGING TO SELL

Up until now, I have written about Staging homes to sell. This may be the heart of the industry, but it is not where it stops. I predict substantial growth in seven other arenas:

1. Staging to Live.
2. Staging to Work.
3. Staging for events.
4. Staging public spaces.
5. Staging commercial properties to sell or rent.
6. Staging for builders.
7. Staging for seniors.

Staging to Live is helping people who have recently moved or who want to simplify their lives by Staging their living space. A clean, clutterfree home that is painted in soothing colors is less stressful than a crowded, chaotic house. The question is how does Staging to Sell a property translate to Staging to Live?

The scenario I see most often is one that I share with ASP Stagers during their training. A husband comes home one day and tells his wife about a lucrative job transfer to Texas. (This could be a wife telling a husband, but I will stay with the traditional construct for efficiency.) The wife is reluctant at first. She looks around the home she has lovingly created and feels wistful. Her husband entices her with the prospect of a larger house, more income, and the promise to fly the grandkids down on holidays and vacations. She agrees in the end, recalling that a few months earlier when she suggested that they redecorate the living room, her husband vetoed the idea. Now, in her new house in Dallas, she will be able to create the living room she wants.

A few days later, the husband comes home from a trip to Dallas. He mentions to his wife that he read about something called "Home Staging" in a magazine on the plane. Having read the interview with me, he is intrigued by the idea and because he intends to sell their house quickly, he suggests that his wife track down an ASP Stager to prepare the house for sale.

The Staging produces two results. First, the house sells in just a few days and for the asking price. Second, and perhaps more significant, the wife adores how the Stager has rearranged and streamlined the rooms in her home. "I love this," she tells the Stager. "I wish I could take you to Texas with me to place everything in our new house."

The Stager suggests to the homeowner that she call an ASP Stager in Dallas to Stage her new house "for living." The couple is thrilled by the outcome. He, because the cost is far less than it would be to hire a decorator, and she, because her beloved treasures are showcased and her house looks smashing.

As Stagers, we will be called on with increasing frequency to Stage lived-in homes to enable the homeowners to feel better about their living space. This is not decorating, but a way to work with both homeowners and their home so that they feel positive about their living environment. Decorating is a way to personalize a home; Staging to Sell is depersonalizing it. Staging to Live has a foot in both camps. When you Stage to Live, you respect the homeowners' taste and possessions, but you work with them to create calm, soothing surroundings.

Another winning formula for Staging and a paradigm shift for both selling and decorating, *Staging to Work* represents a natural progression for anyone who has experienced Staging to Live. Because it involves the work space, it is a little different. A company hires a Staging team to streamline the work area to create a tranquil and more productive environment. Stagers who specialize in offices and other work locales will find themselves in high demand once the idea catches on, and that time is drawing near. Stagers will save businesses money in terms of productivity and missed work because serene, well-organized workplaces allow them to function more efficiently. Employees tend to be more industrious in a well-ordered environment.

Staging for events is already catching on in big cities and other places where event planners have taken the concept of a party or business meeting to new heights. These planners currently hire caterers, disc jockeys, florists, and waitstaff. Similarly, they will also come to rely on Stagers to attend to the details of flow, accessibility, comfort zones, and the overall best use of available space. ASP Stagers have been hired to Stage events ranging from weddings and anniversaries to product launch parties for large companies. The clients appreciate the creativity that Stagers bring to the event, and the Stagers enjoy the challenge and the change from Home Staging.

Staging public spaces is a concept that is dear to my heart. We all spend time in public spaces and, whether we realize it or not, we are affected by them. Every September, the International Association of Home Staging Professionals (IAHSP) sponsors a week during which the IAHSP chapters, all consisting of ASP Stagers, volunteer to Stage a shelter, a clinic, a group home, or similar facility in their community. These generous ASP Stagers clear away clutter, reorganize furniture, and hang artwork to make these public spaces inviting, calm, and appealing. While this week is primarily a time to give back to our communities, it has engendered interest in Staging public areas in general. I see this as an idea with enormous potential. Stagers can work in spaces like those mentioned, but also in other public areas such as libraries, parks, train stations, and restaurants. Municipalities and companies that work with the public will discover that it is cost effective to hire Stagers to take a fresh look at their facilities and make them both more functional and more pleasant for all who use them.

Staging commercial properties to sell or rent is a first cousin to Staging homes to sell. If you ever have been involved in leasing a commercial space, you know that there is a need for this service. The successful execution of this kind of Staging will be the subject of another book, but in a nutshell, this concept involves Staging the space to appeal to the widest array of businesses. The office, retail store, or warehouse must look efficient and spacious, and be able to accommodate a specific number of employees, equipment, and furniture. Prospective buyers or tenants will have specific functions in mind for such a space, so the Stager must make sure that the property is clean and clutterfree and that it has been painted, and emptied of anything left behind by the previous tenant—in other words, the place must be ready for any eventuality.

There is tremendous need for commercial Staging, and I predict that the field will grow quickly in coming years, although it will take some work on the part of Stagers to educate commercial real estate professionals about its value. We have achieved far more in the arena of Home Staging, but with the same kind of effort, we will catch up in the commercial sector soon—especially if I have anything to do with it!

Staging for home builders is already happening, and we will see more of it because the days when builders hire decorators to outfit model homes are coming to an end. Decorators tend to overdo. Stagers minimize so that buyers can truly see the space they are buying. Remember: "You can't sell it if you can't see it."

Once they have been educated about the value of Staging, builders are only too happy to hire Stagers rather than decorators. They comprehend that Staging a new house is the most effective way to sell it. Builders are all about selling the space, so Staging makes good sense to them.

Top builders such as Pulte Homes and Remington Homes prove this point. These builders offer to Stage potential buyers' current homes so that they sell quickly and the buyers have more money to invest in one of the builder homes—a brilliant strategy!

This moves the process along. These builders recognize the value of our certification program, and both Pulte and Remington hire only ASPs to Stage for them.

Staging for senior citizens is a concept with enormous potential. It has been estimated that by 2020, 12 million older Americans will require long-term care, and 44 percent of the seniors who own houses will be 75 or older. This means that a lot of folks will need help selling their homes and downsizing to small spaces. I predict that Stagers will fill an important role here. Not only will they help seniors maximize the equity in their homes, but they will also be trained to help them over many of the hurdles that come with every real estate transaction. In addition, Stagers can benefit seniors when they move into smaller houses, condominiums, or assisted-living apartments. Having a well-ordered home is never more important than when you make a major life change, and the senior market will welcome Stagers and all we can do to help them make these transitions during their later years.

This was brought home for me by Wendy Whitehead, an ASP Stager from the Toronto, Canada area, who wrote me about Staging a room in an assisted-living facility. Her mother-in-law had to move directly from the hospital to the facility, leaving behind her house and all her possessions. "Had I picked the right items, accessories, artwork, and, more important, pictures? Would she feel at home?" Wendy wondered. When she and her husband brought her mother-in-law to the room, Wendy recalled that her heart sank. Would she look at the room as "just that or the home I had tried to make? She turned to me, smiled, and hugged me as tightly as she could. 'This is the best homecoming I've ever had; it's perfect! It must have been so hard for you to go through my things and I so love and appreciate that you cared enough to make this room so special." Wendy believes that without her ASP training she would not have been able to look at the project as impartially as she needed to in order to make the room feel like home. "It was the hardest Staging project I had ever done, but it gave me the biggest reward," she said.

Because of the terrific need for Staging that exists with the senior population, I have opened a senior division at Staged-Homes.com, which can be accessed at SeniorStages.com. Check it out! There you will learn more about earning the designation of Certified Relocation Transition Specialist (CRTS). As the population ages, the need for helping seniors with transitions in their lives is a growing one. Those who like to serve seniors have a wonderful future, too.

THE BEST IS YET TO COME

As anyone who has taken my ASP course, watched my DVDs, or seen me on television knows, I am a happy, optimistic person. I leap headlong into everything I do with enthusiasm and joy!

I created Home Staging in 1972 as a way to help sell the real estate that I listed, and I was thrilled when the concept started to catch on with other real estate agents. When I had the opportunity in 1985 to travel the country to speak and educate the real estate community about Home Staging, I dedicated myself to the mission. I worked extremely hard to become the best speaker I could be. Before long, I thought nothing of standing up in front of hundreds or even thousands of people to teach them that Staging every home was the way to go. The promoters who sponsored these speaking events calculate that I addressed more than a million people during those years. This has enabled me to spread the word about Home Staging across North America, and now the world.

These days, two things thrill me more than anything: speaking to a roomful of eager, excited future ASP Home Stagers and Staging a property. The people who come to hear me when I speak clearly can't wait to learn what I know and apply it to their own existing or future businesses. To me, that is an incredible rush! When I Stage a house, I push up my sleeves and immerse myself in the creative process of Staging. I love the process of Staging a wonderful home that I know in my heart will sell like hotcakes once it's done.

As happy as Staging and training others to Stage make me, what is most gratifying is that so many lives have changed for the better because of Staging. It's a winning strategy if ever there was one, and it will only get better as time goes by.

When more stagers and real estate agents earn their ASP designations, when more homeowners experience firsthand successful sales as a result of Staging, and when more Stagers make a respectable living doing what they love, the world will be a better place. Everyone involved in Home Staging is a winner, and they bring peace to the properties they deal with as well. Whether you Stage to Sell, Stage to Live, or Stage in one of the other ways I've outlined here, the process brings joy and delight to all.

This is why I can say with all my heart and soul that the best is yet to come.

Thank you for reading my book and for being interested in Home Staging. I wish you happy Staging and happy living as you go about your days in the way you want. I ask you to create a better place in the world by living your dreams. Life has so much to offer when you do!

I will continue to work with and teach anyone who wants to hear my message and help me carry out my mission of making the world a better place to live and work through the magic of Home Staging.

Blessings to you all!

Barb's Staging Resource Center

More than anything, I want you to find pleasure in your new business. Home Staging is one of the most enjoyable careers there is, but if you don't pay attention to legal and financial realities, your bliss could turn into a major headache.

Appendix A presents a few standard forms to give you an idea of what is involved when you enter into agreements with clients. These are for educational purposes only; *they are not meant to be copied verbatim.* Appendix B gives you projections of how much real estate agents can earn when they Stage listed homes. You can use this information in marketing your Home Staging service to them. Appendix C offers instructions to homeowners on how to show their property to best advantage to prospective buyers. Appendix D lists the criteria to use when Staging a home. Appendix E is a checklist for homeowners to assist them in them in the moving process. And, finally, Appendix F is a list of the IAHSP chapters throughout North America and includes contact information for me and my company, StagedHomes.com.

Hire an attorney. It is important to be sure that all the information you use—including the information presented here—is accurate, because laws change frequently, as do fees, forms, and procedures in your city/county/state/province/country. We do not guarantee that the information contained here is up to date, including the articles and sample agreements (collectively the "materials"), and we specifically disclaim any warranties respecting the accuracy, completeness, or currency of the materials provided. The materials provided herein are provided "as is" and "without warranty of any kind" expressed or implied (including without limitation, any implied warranty of merchantability or fitness for a particular purpose).

As with any new business venture, you should always consult your own attorney and insurance and tax advisor(s) licensed in your area prior to beginning your Home Staging business. This is the only smart way to begin and continue to grow your business.

NOTICE: *The following materials are provided for general informational purposes and constitute neither exhaustive study nor legal, tax, or insurance advice. They are often presented in summary or aggregate form. They are not meant as a substitute for the advice provided by your own attorney or insurance and tax professionals licensed in your area. The information and materials are not intended to provide legal advice for you to rely on, and your use, if any, does not create any attorney-client relationship of any kind. Applicability to any particular situation is dependent on many factors, including variations of the laws in your area addressed to a specific set of known facts. Do not use this information as a substitute for obtaining professional advice from an attorney, insurance professional, and tax advisor licensed in your city/county/state/province/country.*

APPENDIX A

SAMPLE DOCUMENTS

SAMPLE DOCUMENT 1

Home Staging Services Agreement

This Agreement for Home Staging Services at _____ [Address] (the "Property") is made as of [date] by and between _____, owner of the Property and a resident of [your State] ("Client") and _____ a [your State] corporation ("Staging Company") Or, if you have not incorporated your business [your name d/b/a[name of business]], a resident of [your State] ("_____" you can use "Stager" or your initials, your last name, your d/b/a, etc., to refer to you).

A. Description of Services

Example 1

Subject to the terms and conditions of this Agreement, [Staging Company] agrees to provide Home Staging Services at the Property, including

(continued)

but not limited to furniture arrangement, organization, clutter elimination, and enhancement [optional with furnishings, accessories, and props rented by client] for the purposes of Staging said Property.

Example 2
Professional Services: Upon the terms described herein, [Staging Company] agrees to Stage the Property at the above address. Areas to be Staged shall include [list rooms] and shall exclude [list rooms excluded from Staging].

Optional: If you prepare a written Staging consultation and the client wants you to execute the Staging recommendations, instead of summarizing your Staging Services in the Agreement you may attach the written consultation as an addendum or exhibit to your Contract (e.g., Exhibit A, Addendum 1) and have the client initial all pages of the exhibit or addendum.

B. Payment

Example 1
Client will pay to [Staging Company] the sum of $_____ for the Home Staging Services. Payment is due in full [choose one: upon signing this Agreement or upon completion of Staging Services].

Example 2
Client will pay to [Staging Company] the sum of $_____ for Staging the Property. An initial nonrefundable payment of $_____ is due upon signing this Agreement and the remainder is due upon completion of the Staging Services.

Example 3 Home Staging Written Consultation Services
Client shall compensate [Staging Company] as follows: a payment of $_____ shall be made payable upon execution of this Agreement. If Client requests, [Staging Company] can be hired for further Staging Services and to execute the recommendations in the written Staging consultation report for an additional fee that will be based upon the scope of work to be done.

Optional: Additional Payment Terms (Based on Your Policies for Your Business)

Example 1:

Staging Fees are due and payable in full prior to the Staging date [or upon completion of Staging Services]. Staging Services canceled within _____ days of the Staging date will be assessed 50 percent of the total Staging Fee. A Staging date will be confirmed once the bid is approved by Client.

Example 2

The Staging Fee does not include storage/moving materials. Client agrees to provide at no cost to [Staging Company] all such materials including but not limited to: packing boxes, bubble wrap, packing material and tape, and marking pens.

C. Client Consent

Client hereby grants to [Staging Company] and its employees, agents, independent contractors, and suppliers permission to enter upon and use the Property for the purpose of providing Home Staging Services listed above, beginning on [date] and continuing until completed.

Client agrees to protect any and all valuables in or about the Property by removing them to safe storage before [date of Staging].

Client acknowledges and agrees that Client's belongings may or may not be moved from room to room, or rearranged, or removed for storage (in the garage or off-site) at the sole discretion of [Staging Company]. Client further acknowledges and agrees that [Staging Company] may use nails or other similar materials to hang or display accessories as part of the Home Staging Services.

Client hereby grants permission to [Staging Company] for anything on the Property (both interior and exterior) to be moved or rearranged inside or outside, including furniture or items from cupboards, pantries,

(continued)

closets, drawers, and the like as [Staging Company] deems necessary in its sole discretion to prepare the Property for sale except for the following item(s):

_____

_____

_____

D. Release and Waiver

Assumption of Risk
Example 1
Client acknowledges and agrees that installation of mirrors, artwork, wall hangings, and other furnishings during the Staging process may require hooks and/or nails to be placed in the walls of Property. Upon removal, small holes will be left. Touch-up work on these is the responsibility of Client.

Example 2
Client assumes all responsibility for personal property and for any markings or holes from artwork and/or furnishings incurred during installation, display, and/or removal throughout the Staging process.

Hold Harmless
Example 1
Client further agrees to release, indemnify, and hold harmless [Staging Company], its officers, employees, agents, contractors, and suppliers ("Releasees") against any and all losses, liabilities, damages, injuries, expenses, and claims (including reasonable attorney's fees) of Client or any third party arising from Releasees' entry onto the Property and/or activities as authorized by this Agreement, whether caused by negligence or otherwise, including without limitation property damage and personal injury claims.

Example 2

Client further agrees to release, indemnify, and hold harmless [Staging Company], its officers, employees, agents, contractors, and suppliers against any and all losses, accidents, liabilities, damages, injuries, expenses, and claims resulting in whole or part, directly or indirectly, from the Staging process.

Example 3

[Staging Company] is not liable for any personal injury or property damage resulting in whole or part, directly or indirectly, from the Staging process and/or from any use of rented furnishings, and Client acknowledges and agrees to assume any such risk.

E. Limitation of Liability

Example 1

CLIENT HEREBY AGREES THAT IN NO EVENT SHALL [Staging Company]'s, ITS OFFICERS', EMPLOYEES', AGENTS', CONTRACTORS', AND/OR SUPPLIERS' TOTAL AND AGGREGATE LIABILITY UNDER THIS AGREEMENT EXCEED THE AMOUNT OF FEES PAID BY CLIENT.

Example 2

CLIENT AGREES THAT [Staging Company]'s TOTAL LIABILITY IS LIMITED TO A REFUND OF THE FEE ACTUALLY PAID FOR THE HOME STAGING SERVICES. THE LIABILITY OF [Staging Company]'s PRINCIPALS, EMPLOYEES, AGENTS, CONTRACTORS, AND SUPPLIERS IS ALSO LIMITED TO THE FEE PAID BY CLIENT.

Optional: Absence of Warranties/Guarantees

Example 1

Client understands that [Staging Company] does not and cannot guarantee success or any particular result. While we shall use our best professional efforts to achieve a successful result, we can make no warranty or guarantee expressed or implied as to the successful sale of the Property in your favor. An expression of the relative merits of the Property and your chances of success are only expressions of opinion and estimates.

(continued)

Example 2

By performing Home Staging Consultation Services, [Staging Company] shall use good faith best efforts to present the Property in the best possible manner to potential buyers. [Staging Company] does not guarantee that the Property will sell faster, or at the highest market value, and is not responsible for the final outcome of any sale of the Property.

Example 3

Home Staging is a marketing tool to prepare a home for sale. This is not a home warranty, assessment, appraisal, guarantee expressed or implied, insurance policy, or substitute for real estate transfer disclosures which may be required by law.

F. Photography and Publicity Release

Example 1

Client agrees to allow [Staging Company] to photograph Staged areas of the Property before and after the work is completed and to use all such photographs for reference and marketing purposes. Client's name will not be referenced.

Example 2

[Staging Company] shall have the right to photograph and otherwise record the Property (interior and exterior) before and after the provision of Staging Services (collectively the "Likeness") and use and reuse all such photographs and recordings in any media now known or hereafter developed worldwide in perpetuity for advertising, trade, promotion, and publicity purposes without further notification or permission and with no remuneration to Client. Client agrees [Staging Company] may use all or part of the Likeness and may alter or modify it regardless of whether the Property is identifiable. Client further agrees that [Staging Company] owns all right, title, and interest (including without limitation all copyrights) in all such photographs and recordings hereunder and releases [Staging Company] from any claims or liability arising out of the recording or use thereof.

G. Optional Standard Terms

Insurance

Example 1

Client agrees to obtain and/or maintain his or her own personal property loss insurance.

Example 2

Client agrees to have all personal property adequately insured throughout the Staging process.

Example 3

[Staging Company] shall provide proof of its own business liability insurance per Client request.

Advertising

Client acknowledges and agrees that [Staging Company] may reasonably advertise [Staging Company]'s services in the Property while the Property remains Staged.

Pre-Stage Cleaning

Client agrees to have the Property, including carpeting and windows, professionally cleaned prior to [the Staging date].

H. General Provisions

Governing Law

This Agreement shall be governed by the laws of the State of [Your State].

Entire Agreement

Example 1

This Agreement contains the entire agreement of the parties, and there are no other promises or conditions in any other agreement whether oral or written.

(continued)

Example 2

This Agreement and the documents referred to herein (if any) constitute the entire Agreement between the parties hereto, and supersede any and all prior representations, discussions, or agreements whether oral or written.

Optional General Provisions

Attachments and Exhibits

All attachments and exhibits referred to in this Agreement are incorporated herein by reference.

Ownership of the Property

Client warrants that Client is the owner of record of the Property and has the right and authority to make and enter into this Agreement and to grant the rights set forth herein. Client acknowledges and agrees that no other authorization is necessary to enable [Staging Company] to use the Property for the purposes herein contemplated.

Severability

If any provision of this Agreement is invalid or unenforceable, the remainder of this Agreement shall nevertheless remain in full force and effect and shall be construed as if the unenforceable portion(s) were deleted.

Signatures

Example 1

ACCEPTED AND AGREED THIS _____ day of _____, 20[   ]

Client/Property Owner	Staging Company
By _____	By _____
Printed Name_____	Printed Name_____
Date_____	Date_____
Address_____	Address_____
_____	_____
_____	_____

Example 2

By signing below, Client agrees to pay [Staging Company] the above fees in full upon completion of Staging [or before Staging date].

ACCEPTED AND AGREED THIS _____ day of _____, 20[   ]

Client/Property Owner	Staging Company
By _____	By _____
Printed Name_____	Printed Name_____
Date_____	Date_____
Address_____	Address_____
_____	_____
_____	_____

Example 3

Each party represents and warrants that on this date they are duly authorized to bind their respective principals by their signatures below.

ACCEPTED AND AGREED THIS _____ day of _____, 20[   ]

Client/Property Owner	Staging Company
By _____	By _____
Printed Name_____	Printed Name_____
Date_____	Date_____
Address_____	Address_____
_____	_____
_____	_____

Example 4

YOU SHOULD READ AND UNDERSTAND THIS AGREEMENT. IT IS A LEGAL AND BINDING CONTRACT. Signing below means you have read the Staging Agreement, are in full agreement with it and have received a copy of the fully executed Staging Agreement.

ACCEPTED AND AGREED THIS _____ day of _____, 20[   ]

Client/Property Owner	Staging Company
By _____	By _____
Printed Name_____	Printed Name_____
Date_____	Date_____
Address_____	Address_____
_____	_____
_____	_____

SAMPLE DOCUMENT 2

Furniture and Accessories Rental Agreement

This Agreement for the rental [or lease] of furniture and accessories for purposes of Staging the residence located at _____ [Address] (hereafter the "Property") is made as of [date] by and between _____, owner of the Property and a resident of [State] (hereafter "Client"), and _____, a [your State] corporation (hereafter "Staging Company"). Or, if you have not incorporated your business [your name d/b/a [name of business]], a resident of [your State] (hereafter "_____" you can use "Stager" or your initials, your last name, your d/b/a, etc., to refer to you).

A. Description of Services/Furnishings and Accessories Inventory

Example 1

Description of Services: Attached as Exhibit A is a list [or inventory] of furniture and/or decorative accessories ("Furnishings") owned by [Staging Company] and leased to Client under the terms and conditions contained herein for purposes of Staging the Property. Client will sign an acknowledgment of inventory provided by [Staging Company] upon completion of installation and Staging Services.

Example 2

[Staging Company] shall, during the course of this Agreement, rent to Client home furnishings, plants, and/or accessories (collectively "Furnishings") listed on the attached Inventory for [rooms/areas to be Staged]. [Areas/rooms not Staged] will not be included unless otherwise noted in this Agreement.

Example 3

Client will sign a written acknowledgment of inventory that will be provided upon completion of installation of furnishings and accessories to be attached as Exhibit A. [Staging Company] requires a five-day period of notice to remove our furniture and accessories from the Property.

B. Payment and Term

Example 1

The monthly rental fee for the Furnishings leased by [Staging Company] and installed in the Property is $_____. [Staging Company] will invoice Client on the 25th of each month for the next month's rental. Rental fees are due in advance and are not prorated if the Furnishings are removed before month's end. A minimum of one week's advance notice to [Staging Company] is required to schedule removal of the Furnishings.

Example 2

The Furnishings described in attachment will be rented at a rate of $_____ per month on a month-to-month basis. The rental fees for the Furnishings are nonrefundable and are due and payable on or before the ____th day of every month. The rental fee will be charged in advance and for each successive monthly rental period. The rental term will renew automatically month-to-month on the ____th day of the month unless canceled ____ days in advance. If ____ days' notice prior to the upcoming monthly payment are not given, Client will be required to pay the next month's rental fee. Fees are not prorated.

C. Damage or Loss to Furniture and Accessories

Example 1

Client agrees to maintain the Furnishings in good repair and operating condition and to return all items to [Staging Company] in the condition received, excluding normal wear and tear. Client will be responsible for any damage or loss to furniture or accessories while installed on the premises. [Optional: Client agrees that for purposes of this Agreement, replacement value for the Furnishings shall be $_____.]

Example 2

Client agrees to exercise all due care in keeping, caring for, and preserving the Furnishings. Client shall remain responsible for all damage to the Furnishings while they are at the Property, up to and including actual replacement value for each damaged and missing item.

(continued)

Example 3

As the homeowner for the Property, Client hereby assumes all liability for the cost of repairing or replacing any damaged, lost, or stolen piece of the leased furniture and/or accessories. [Staging Company] will charge Client by invoice and Client agrees to pay for the cost of replacing each damaged, lost, or stolen item.

Example 4

Client acknowledges and agrees that the Furnishings and accessories listed on the Inventory attached as Exhibit A are owned and leased by [Staging Company] for display purposes only while the Property remains Staged and are not to be used in any other fashion. [Optional: Client further acknowledges and agrees that the Furnishings shall remain at the Property during the term of this Agreement and shall not be removed from the Property except by [Staging Company]]. Client hereby assumes all liability for the cost of repairing or replacing any damaged, lost, or stolen piece of the leased furniture and/or accessories. [Staging Company] will charge Client by invoice and Client agrees to pay for the cost of replacing each damaged, lost, or stolen item.

D. Termination; Default

This Agreement may be terminated by either Party upon 14 days' written or verbal notice to the other Party. Notwithstanding the foregoing, in the event of Default [Staging Company] may terminate this Agreement without notice and may immediately remove all Furnishings; Client remains obligated to pay all unpaid fees and costs accrued through and including the final monthly rental period. Default occurs when Client fails to fulfill or abide by any obligations or terms under this Agreement, including non-payment of fees and costs.

Upon termination of this Agreement, Client shall voluntarily surrender the Furnishings to [Staging Company] in the same condition as they were when received by Client, although ordinary wear and tear is accepted.

E. Client Consent

Client hereby grants to [Staging Company] and its employees, agents, independent contractors, and suppliers permission to enter upon and use the Property for the purpose of providing Home Staging Services listed above beginning on [date] and continuing until completed.

Client agrees to protect any and all valuables in or about the Property by removing them to safe storage before [date of Staging].

Client acknowledges and agrees that Client's belongings may or may not be moved from room to room, or rearranged, or removed for storage (in the garage or off-site) at the sole discretion of [Staging Company]. Client further acknowledges and agrees that [Staging Company] may use nails or other similar materials to hang or display accessories as part of the Home Staging Services.

Client hereby grants permission to [Staging Company] for anything on the Property (both interior and exterior) to be moved or rearranged inside or outside, including furniture or items from cupboards, pantries, closets, drawers, and the like, as [Staging Company] deems necessary in its sole discretion to prepare the Property for sale except for the following item(s):

_____

_____

_____

F. Release and Waiver

Assumption of Risk

Example 1

Client assumes all responsibility for personal property and for any markings or holes from artwork and/or Furnishings incurred during installation, display, and/or removal throughout the Staging process.

(continued)

Example 2

Client acknowledges and agrees that [Staging Company] is not liable for any personal injury or property damage during installation, use, and/or removal of the Furnishings and accessories.

Client acknowledges and agrees that installation of mirrors, artwork, wall hangings, and other Furnishings during the Staging process may require hooks and/or nails to be placed in the walls of property. Upon removal, small holes will be left. Touch-up work on these is the responsibility of Client.

G. Hold Harmless

Example 1

Client further agrees to release, indemnify, and hold harmless [Staging Company], its officers, employees, agents, contractors, and suppliers ("Releasees") against any and all losses, liabilities, damages, injuries, expenses, and claims (including reasonable attorney's fees) of Client or any third party arising from Releasees' entry onto the Property and/or activities as authorized by this Agreement, whether caused by negligence or otherwise, including without limitation property damage and personal injury claims.

Example 2

Client further agrees to release, indemnify, and hold harmless [Staging Company], its officers, employees, agents, contractors, and suppliers against any and all losses, accidents, liabilities, damages, injuries, expenses, and claims resulting in whole or part, directly or indirectly, from the Staging process.

Example 3

[Staging Company] is not liable for any personal injury or property damage resulting in whole or part, directly or indirectly, from the Staging process and/or from any use of rented furnishings, and Client acknowledges and agrees to assume any such risk.

H. Limitation of Liability

Example 1

CLIENT HEREBY AGREES THAT IN NO EVENT SHALL [Staging Company]'s, ITS OFFICERS', EMPLOYEES', AGENTS', CONTRACTORS', AND/OR SUPPLIERS' TOTAL AND AGGREGATE LIABILITY UNDER THIS AGREEMENT EXCEED THE AMOUNT OF FEES PAID BY CLIENT.

Example 2

CLIENT AGREES THAT [Staging Company]'s TOTAL LIABILITY IS LIMITED TO A REFUND OF THE FEE ACTUALLY PAID FOR THE HOME STAGING SERVICES. THE LIABILITY OF [Staging Company]'s PRINCIPALS, EMPLOYEES, AGENTS, CONTRACTORS, AND SUPPLIERS IS ALSO LIMITED TO THE FEE PAID BY CLIENT.

I. [Optional] Absence of Warranties/Guarantees

Example 1

Client understands that [Staging Company] does not and cannot guarantee success or any particular result. While we shall use our best professional efforts to achieve a successful result, we can make no warranty or guarantee expressed or implied as to the successful sale of the Property in your favor. An expression of the relative merits of the Property and your chances of success are only expressions of opinion and estimates.

Example 2

By performing Home Staging Consultation Services, [Staging Company] shall use good faith best efforts to present the Property in the best possible manner to potential buyers. [Staging Company] does not guarantee that the Property will sell faster, or at the highest market value, and is not responsible for the final outcome of any sale of the Property.

(continued)

Example 3

Home Staging is a marketing tool to prepare a home for sale. This is not a home warranty, assessment, appraisal, guarantee expressed or implied, insurance policy, or substitute for real estate transfer disclosures which may be required by law.

J. Photography and Publicity Release

Example 1

Client agrees to allow [Staging Company] to photograph Staged areas of the Property before and after the work is completed and to use all such photographs for reference and marketing purposes. Client's name will not be referenced.

Example 2

[Staging Company] shall have the right to photograph and otherwise record the Property (interior and exterior) before and after the provision of Staging Services (collectively the "Likeness") and use and reuse all such photographs and recordings in any media now known or hereafter developed worldwide in perpetuity for advertising, trade, promotion, and publicity purposes without further notification or permission and with no remuneration to Client. Client agrees [Staging Company] may use all or part of the Likeness and may alter or modify it regardless of whether the Property is identifiable. Client further agrees that [Staging Company] owns all right, title, and interest (including without limitation all copyrights) in all such photographs and recordings hereunder and releases [Staging Company] from any claims or liability arising out of the recording or use thereof.

Optional Standard Terms

K. Insurance

Example 1

Client is encouraged to obtain and/or maintain his or her own personal property loss insurance.

Example 2

Client agrees to have all personal property adequately insured throughout the Staging process.

Example 3

[Staging Company] shall provide proof of liability insurance per Client request.

L. Advertising

Client acknowledges and agrees that [Staging Company] may reasonably advertise [Staging Company]'s services in the Property while the Property remains Staged.

M. Pre-Stage Cleaning

Client agrees to have the Property, including carpeting and windows, professionally cleaned prior to [the Staging date].

N. General Provisions

Governing Law

This Agreement shall be governed by the laws of the State of [Your State].

Entire Agreement

Example 1

This Agreement contains the entire agreement of the parties, and there are no other promises or conditions in any other agreement whether oral or written.

Example 2

This Agreement and the documents referred to herein (if any) constitute the entire Agreement between the parties hereto, and supersede any and all prior representations, discussions, or agreements whether oral or written.

(continued)

O. Optional General Provisions

Attachments and Exhibits

All attachments and exhibits referred to in this Agreement are incorporated herein by reference.

Ownership of the Property

Client warrants that Client is the owner of record of the Property and has the right and authority to make and enter into this Agreement and to grant the rights set forth herein. Client acknowledges and agrees that no other authorization is necessary to enable [Staging Company] to use the Property for the purposes herein contemplated.

Severability

If any provision of this Agreement is invalid or unenforceable, the remainder of this Agreement shall nevertheless remain in full force and effect and shall be construed as if the unenforceable portion(s) were deleted.

P. Signatures

Example 1

ACCEPTED AND AGREED THIS _____ day of _____, 20[   ]

Client/Property Owner	Staging Company
By _____	By _____
Printed Name_____	Printed Name_____
Date_____	Date_____
Address_____	Address_____
_____	_____
_____	_____

Example 2

By signing below, Client agrees to pay [Staging Company] the above fees in full upon completion of Staging [or before Staging date].

ACCEPTED AND AGREED THIS _____ day of _____, 20[   ]

Client/Property Owner	Staging Company
By _____	By _____

Printed Name_____   Printed Name_____

Date_____   Date_____

Address_____   Address_____

_____   _____

_____   _____

Example 3

Each party represents and warrants that on this date they are duly authorized to bind their respective principals by their signatures below.

ACCEPTED AND AGREED THIS ____ day of _____, 20[   ]

Client/Property Owner   Staging Company

By _____   By _____

Printed Name_____   Printed Name_____

Date_____   Date_____

Address_____   Address_____

_____   _____

_____   _____

Example 4

YOU SHOULD READ AND UNDERSTAND THIS AGREEMENT. IT IS A LEGAL AND BINDING CONTRACT. Signing below means you have read the Staging Agreement, are in full agreement with it, and have received a copy of the fully executed Staging Agreement.

ACCEPTED AND AGREED THIS _____ day of _____, 20[   ]

Client/Property Owner   Staging Company

By _____   By _____

Printed Name_____   Printed Name_____

Date_____   Date_____

Address_____   Address_____

_____   _____

_____   _____

SAMPLE DOCUMENT 3

Homeowner Agreement

Date of Staging _____

Name of Property Owner(s) _____

The "Property" _____

Address of Property to Be Staged _____

_____

A. Written Bid/Proposal for Home Staging Services

[Staging Company] hereby agrees to provide Home Staging Services at the Property per this Homeowner Agreement and the written bid/proposal incorporated by reference and subject to payment of all fees and costs.

B. Client Consent

Client hereby grants to [Staging Company], and its employees, agents, independent contractors, and suppliers, permission to enter upon and use the Property for the purpose of providing Home Staging Services beginning on [date] and continuing until completed.

Client agrees to protect any and all valuables in or about the Property by removing them to safe storage before [date of Staging].

Client agrees to provide at no cost to [Staging Company] all storage/ moving materials including but not limited to: packing boxes, bubble wrap, packing material and tape, and marking pens.

Client acknowledges and agrees that Client's belongings may or may not be moved from room to room, or rearranged, or removed for storage (in the garage or off-site) at the sole discretion of [Staging Company]. Client further acknowledges and agrees that [Staging Company] may use nails or other similar materials to hang or display accessories as part of the Home Staging Services.

Client hereby grants permission to [Staging Company] for anything on the Property (both interior and exterior) to be moved or rearranged inside or outside, including furniture or items from cupboards, pantries, closets, drawers, and the like as [Staging Company] deems necessary in its sole discretion to prepare the Property for sale except for the following item(s):

_____

_____

_____

C. Photography and Publicity Release

Example 1

Client agrees to allow [Staging Company] to photograph Staged areas of the Property before and after the work is completed and to use all such photographs for reference and marketing purposes. [Optional Client's name will not be referenced.]

Example 2

[Staging Company] shall have the right to photograph and otherwise record the Property (interior and exterior) before and after the provision of Staging Services (collectively the "Likeness") and use and reuse all such photographs and recordings in any media now known or hereafter developed worldwide in perpetuity for advertising, trade, promotion, and publicity purposes without further notification or permission and with no remuneration to Client. Client agrees [Staging Company] may use all or part of the Likeness and may alter or modify it regardless of whether the Property is identifiable. Client further agrees that [Staging Company] owns all right, title, and interest (including without limitation all copyrights) in all such photographs and recordings hereunder and releases

(continued)

[Staging Company] from any claims or liability arising out of the recording or use thereof.

D. Release and Waiver

Assumption of Risk
Example 1
Client assumes all responsibility for personal property and for any markings or holes from artwork and/or Furnishings incurred during installation, display, and/or removal throughout the Staging process.

Example 2
Client acknowledges and agrees that [Staging Company] is not liable for any personal injury or property damage during installation, use, and/or removal of the Furnishings and accessories.

Client acknowledges and agrees that installation of mirrors, artwork, wall hangings, and other Furnishings during the Staging process may require hooks and/or nails to be placed in the walls of property. Upon removal, small holes will be left. Touch-up work on these is the responsibility of Client.

E. Hold Harmless

Example 1
Client further agrees to release, indemnify, and hold harmless [Staging Company], its officers, employees, agents contractors, and suppliers ("Releasees") against any and all losses, liabilities, damages, injuries, expenses, and claims (including reasonable attorney's fees) of Client or any third party arising from Releasees' entry onto the Property and/or activities as authorized by this Agreement, whether caused by negligence or otherwise, including without limitation property damage and personal injury claims.

Example 2
Client further agrees to release, indemnify, and hold harmless [Staging Company], its officers, employees, agents, contractors, and suppliers

against any and all losses, accidents, liabilities, damages, injuries, expenses, and claims resulting in whole or part, directly or indirectly, from the Staging process.

Example 3

[Staging Company] is not liable for any personal injury or property damage resulting in whole or part, directly or indirectly, from the Staging process and/or from any use of rented Furnishings, and Client acknowledges and agrees to assume any such risk.

E. Limitation of Liability

Example 1

CLIENT HEREBY AGREES THAT IN NO EVENT SHALL [Staging Company]'s, ITS OFFICERS', EMPLOYEES', AGENTS', CONTRACTORS', AND/OR SUPPLIERS' TOTAL AND AGGREGATE LIABILITY UNDER THIS AGREEMENT EXCEED THE AMOUNT OF FEES PAID BY CLIENT.

Example 2

CLIENT AGREES THAT [Staging Company]'s TOTAL LIABILITY IS LIMITED TO A REFUND OF THE FEE ACTUALLY PAID FOR THE HOME STAGING SERVICES. THE LIABILITY OF [Staging Company]'s PRINCIPALS, EMPLOYEES, AGENTS, CONTRACTORS, AND SUPPLIERS IS ALSO LIMITED TO THE FEE PAID BY CLIENT.

Optional: Absence of Warranties/Guarantees

Example 1

Client understands that [Staging Company] does not and cannot guarantee success or any particular result. While we shall use our best professional efforts to achieve a successful result, we can make no warranty or guarantee expressed or implied as to the successful sale of the Property in your favor. Any expression of the relative merits of the Property and your chances of success are only expressions of opinion and estimates.

(continued)

Example 2

By performing Home Staging Consultation Services, [Staging Company] shall use good faith best efforts to present the Property in the best possible manner to potential buyers. [Staging Company] does not guarantee that the Property will sell faster, or at the highest market value, and is not responsible for the final outcome of any sale of the Property.

Example 3

Home Staging is a marketing tool to prepare a home for sale. This is not a home warranty, assessment, appraisal, guarantee expressed or implied, insurance policy, or substitute for real estate transfer disclosures which may be required by law.

ACCEPTED AND AGREED THIS _____ day of _____, 20[ ]

Property Owner(s)   Property Owner(s)

By _____   By _____

Printed Name_____   Printed Name_____

Date_____   Date_____

Address_____   Address_____

_____   _____

_____   _____

Staging Company

By _____

Printed Name_____

Date_____

Address_____

_____

_____

SAMPLE STAGING INVENTORY OF FURNITURE AND ACCESSORIES

Leased by [Staging Company] and Placed in the Property

The "Property"

Address: _____

_____

Staging Date: _____

Client: _____

Front Entry
1 black-and-white mat
1 white table

Living Room and Dining Room
1 black floor lamp
1 glass plate with potpourri
2 black pillows—cotton
1 lamp—brass/reading

Hall—Downstairs
1 white table
1 vase—ceramic with contents

Guest Room
2 tables—bedside/wood/covered
2 pillows—1 purple, 1 green
2 king sheets—1 flat, 1 fitted—used as tablecloths
1 mini bench
2 lamps—candlesticks with black shades

Guest Bathroom
1 rug—small oriental green
1 rug—skid
1 shower curtain—green/white leaf print and white rod

(continued)

Downstairs Office
1 office chair
1 basket

Family Room
1 basket by fireplace
1 basket with palm and greens
1 birdhouse—red
1 area rug—green
1 plant stand—iron
1 basket (with owner's plant inside)

Kitchen
1 bistro set—1 table, 2 chairs
1 tablecloth—multicolor with fringe

Upstairs—Two Bedrooms
2 cushions—white
1 lamp—rattan, with shade
2 chairs—rattan
1 throw

Bath—Jack and Jill
2 hand towels—green
1 birdcage with greenery

Upstairs Bathroom
1 black/white—checkered shower curtain

Laundry Room
2 towels—green
1 hand towel
1 lamp
1 small decorative chair
1 plaque

Children's Room
1 rubber ducky
1 picture
1 table
2 chairs

Upstairs Landing
1 tree
Assorted rocks
1 large cottage picture with poppies

Master Bedroom
1 couch—tan with 2 pillows
1 pillow—green
1 throw—green

Master Bath
2 towels—black
1 art deco statuette—woman

Hallway in Master Bedroom
1 mirror—cathedral white
1 basket with greens

Estimated Inventory Replacement Value: $_____

ACCEPTED AND AGREED THIS ____ day of _____, 20[   ]

Property Owner(s)   Property Owner(s)
By _____   By _____
Printed Name_____   Printed Name_____
Date_____   Date_____
Address_____   Address_____
_____   _____
_____   _____

Staging Company
By _____
Printed Name_____
Date_____
Address_____
_____
_____

SAMPLE RENTAL INVOICE

DATE
INVOICE # 101
10/25/06
BILL TO
DELIVER TO
Jane Doe
1234 Main St.
Anytown, CA 12345

DUE DATE
P.O. #

ITEM
DESCRIPTION
QUANTITY
RATE
AMOUNT

Table runner
Burgundy/green
1
$8.00
$8.00

Café table
Black/folding
1
$8.00
$8.00

Rose Topiary
Yellow 12 inches
1
$3.00

Lamp
Silver
1
$10.00
$10.00

Accent pillows
Beige/green/pineapple
3
$2.00
$6.00

Art
Italian country
1
$10.00
$10.00

SUBTOTAL
$45
TOTAL
$45

APPENDIX B

INCREASING REAL ESTATE AGENT EARNINGS THROUGH STAGING

How much can real estate agents earn when they have their listings Staged? An estimated $48,000, or even more. Tell them about it.

When you talk to real estate agents, tell them about the projections shown here. National statistics indicate that Staged homes net 3 to 10 percent more on average than homes that are not Staged. If the median price of a home is $241,000,* the following calculations can be made for real estate agents. (For markets where the median home price is double this amount, double the figures given. Of course, nothing is certain, but keep in mind that Staging is a value-added service.)

If an agent sells a $241,000 home for 3 to 10 percent more, this equates to a $7,230 to $24,100 equity gain, or an average of $15,665.[†]

*Based on national statistics for median-priced home sales from January 2005.
[†] Based on a statistical study from 2004–2005 of Staged properties nationwide.

- At 3 percent commission, this is $470 more for the agent per sale.

If the agent sells two to four homes per month . . .

- At 3 percent commission, this is $940 to $1,880 more for the agent per month.

And that means:

- At 3 percent commission, $11,280 to $22,560 more per year that the agent could earn in commissions, based on this low median selling price of $241,000.

For example, if an agent offers sellers the possibility of getting at least 3 percent more for their home by Staging it, don't you think they would be willing to pay the full commission to the listing agent? The agent is adding more value, so the clients will make a lot more as a result.

OTHER BENEFITS

When listings sell faster, agents don't have to market them for as long—and that is a cost saving to them. It means less newspaper advertising, lower marketing costs, less time spent at open houses, fewer brochures produced, and so on.

Advertising costs average a minimum of $700 per transaction.

- $700 × 3 transactions = $2,100 per month × 12 = $25,200!

When you add the extra commission dollars earned and the expense dollars saved, as the preceding example shows, it is clear that real estate agents come out ahead by Staging their listings, potentially earning another $48,000 or more a year ($22,560 extra in commissions + $25,200 in expense savings = $47,760).

Furthermore, what about the new business you will bring in as a result of using Staging to gain listings? How much more can you earn? Thousands more . . . and the best part is that the sellers benefit, too!

This example was originally prepared for StagedHomes.com by Jennie Norris, ASPM, IAHSP.

APPENDIX C

SHOWING INSTRUCTIONS FOR HOMEOWNERS

Stagers should leave a sheet of instructions for homeowners after the property has been Staged. Here is a suggested form.

When real estate agents call to show the house, ask for their names, when they will arrive, and how much time they will require on the premises. Ask them to call if they will be late or have to cancel the appointment. Allow the buyers privacy while they view your home. It is best to leave the premises or work in the yard.

Go through the following checklist before agents and buyers arrive:

- ☐ Open all curtains and blinds, unless otherwise advised.
- ☐ Turn on the lights and lamps designated by the Stager (usually all of them).
- ☐ Close garage doors.
- ☐ Make sure all toilet lids are down.
- ☐ Make sure music is playing softly throughout the house. Soft rock, pop, or light jazz are all appropriate.

Once the house has been shown, call me [the Stager] with the showing agent's name, company, and phone numbers so I can follow up and give you feedback.

You can reach me at my office at: _____
Or call: _____

I appreciate your help in following these instructions as we market your property and work toward a successful sale.

APPENDIX D
STAGING CRITERIA

ASP Stagers can pass this list on to the sellers or keep it for reference when they Stage a property. As we've discussed throughout this book, Staging helps to market the property as a product. Homeowners should understand that this gives them a financial edge and that Staging has nothing to do with personal taste and decorating. As you will explain to them, when the house is Staged, a lot of the inevitable packing, sorting, and discarding is done early.

GENERAL COMMENTS

- Most carpets need to be cleaned. Have yours professionally cleaned.
- Check all light fixtures. Are they working properly? Replace all burned-out lightbulbs. Look for dark hallways and corners and increase the wattage of bulbs in those areas.
- Make sure there are lamps with adequate bulbs in dark corners and that they are turned on for showings.
- Repair and repaint cracks on all walls and ceilings.

- Repair or replace broken light switches and switch plates. Clean any dirty areas around them.
- Keep all curtains and blinds open during the day to let in light and views. The extra expense for additional heating or air-conditioning is a necessary cost of selling.
- Reduce the number of pillows on couches to two or fewer. Remove all afghans and blankets.
- Pack up all valuable items to protect them. If necessary, take them to a safe deposit box.
- Take a hard look at those beloved houseplants. In most cases, they need to be pruned or discarded.
- Fireplaces need to be cleaned out. Glass doors should be cleaned. Mantels and hearths should be cleared off except for a very few necessary items.
- Pack up all collections.
- Reduce the number of books on bookshelves.
- Reduce the number of family pictures on shelves, pianos, and tables.
- Reduce the number of wall-hung photos and paintings in every room to one large piece on a wall or small groups of three. Make sure they are hung at eye level.
- Keep soft music playing at all times for showings.
- Be sensitive to odors, because buyers are. You can't sell it if you can smell it.
- Wash all windows and make sure they open freely. If the seal is broken on a double-pane window, replace it now.
- Repair items that are broken to show that you take care of your home.
- Don't be afraid to move furniture from room to room.
- In general, pack up the little things, which create clutter.

INSIDE OF HOME

Living room, family room, den, or "bonus" room:

- Clear off all coffee tables and end tables and leave only two or three items on each.
- Remove all ashtrays.

Dining room:

- Clear off dining room table except for a single centerpiece.
- Remove tablecloth.
- Remove extra leaves from the table.
- Remove extra dining room chairs. Four or six chairs are enough.
- Clear off the buffet and declutter corner cabinets.

Kitchen:

- Clear off counters. Leave out only what is essential for day-to-day living.
- Leave out a few large, decorative items such as a bowl of fruit.
- Repair any tile or Formica countertops.
- Clean stained tile grout with bleach.
- Remove all magnets, photos, children's drawings, and so on, from the front of the refrigerator.
- Clean the stove top and oven. Replace old burner pans if they are badly stained.
- Clean all exhaust fans, filters, and hoods.
- Clean the kitchen floor and keep it clean for showings.
- Keep the kitchen sink clean and empty on a daily basis.
- Make sure the kitchen faucet does not drip and works smoothly.
- Clear everything off the window ledge above the kitchen sink.
- Pack up the collections in the kitchen, too.

- Remove scatter rugs. Replace with a single, large rug or no rug.
- Empty the garbage regularly to prevent kitchen odors.
- Move dog and cat dishes so they don't interfere with buyers walking around the room.

Bedrooms:

- Make the beds every day.
- Invest in new bedspreads if necessary.
- Clear off bedside tables and chests of drawers except for a very few necessary items.
- Store extra books and magazines underneath the bed.
- Keep closet doors closed. For walk-in closets, keep the floor clean and free of laundry and shoes.
- Reduce the number of photos on tables and chests of drawers to a minimum.
- Take down posters in children's rooms.
- Repair any nail holes and paint the walls, if necessary.

Laundry room:

- Put soaps and cleaners in a cupboard or arrange neatly on a shelf.
- Keep counters and sinks clean and empty.
- Get rid of excess hangers and hanging laundry.

Bathrooms:

- Clear off counters. Leave only essential toiletries out, and arrange them on a tray or in a basket.
- Replace hand soap with a neat bottle of liquid soap.
- Coordinate all towels using one or two colors and hang neatly every day, folded in thirds.

- Clear everything out of the shower and tub except for one bottle of liquid soap and one of shampoo.
- Clean or replace the shower curtain. Keep shower curtains drawn at all times.
- One common problem in a lot of bathrooms is cracking or peeling just above the top of the shower tile or tub enclosure where it meets the drywall or ceiling. Repair using caulking and paint or install wood trim coated in polyurethane.
- Get rid of mold and stains throughout bathroom, especially in the shower and bathtub area.
- Many tubs and showers need a fresh bead of silicone caulking around the edges to make them look neat and clean.
- Take all cloth toilet lid covers and water closet covers off. Keep toilet lids down every day.
- Remove all small rugs. Use only one larger rug, or none.
- Hide cleaning supplies and the trash can under the sink or out of the line of sight.

Hallways and closets:

- Remove any plastic runners in hallways.
- Tidy up closets.
- Make sure nothing falls off the closet shelf when the door is opened.
- Make sure closet doors close easily.

Basements:

- Be aware of unpleasant smells, musty odors, and dampness and alleviate problems by repairing and cleaning problem areas. Use room deodorants and disinfectant sprays to help eliminate any odors.
- Make sure all lighting is in good working order.
- Tidy the basement up and clear away any objects near the furnace and hot water heater.

- Consolidate stored items in one corner of one area of the basement.
- Repair any cracks in the ceilings and walls.
- Clear any drains.

PLACES TO STORE STUFF

- Rent a storage unit.
- Have a garage sale.
- Give it to charity.
- Put it in the attic.
- Store it in the crawl space.
- Use a portion or corner of the basement.
- Use part or all of the garage.
- As a last resort, sacrifice a third or fourth bedroom and fill it full.

Garage or carport:

- Clear everything out of carports.
- Organize garages. Store items neatly in one area.
- Sweep garages.
- Keep garage doors down while your home is on the market.
- Keep cars in the garage if possible.
- Move boats and recreational vehicles to a storage facility or neighbor's property.

OUTSIDE OF HOME

Front door and entry to house:

- Repaint or repair front door and steps.
- Repaint and repair handrails and banisters.
- Trim bushes near front door.

Decks, walkways, porches, and patios:

- Sweep all decks, walkways, porches, and patios, and keep them swept.
- Remove any moss or vines.
- Pressure-wash and stain or paint decks, if they need it.
- Reduce clutter on decks, porches, and patios.
- Get rid of old flowerpots, planters, toys, and construction materials.
- Store the grill and excess furniture.
- Create one simple setting with clean furniture.

Roof and fences:

- Clean all debris and moss from roof and gutters.
- Replace gutters and downspouts, if necessary.
- Repair broken fences and paint, if necessary.

Landscaping:

- Rake and weed flower beds. Mulch or add gravel to make them look neater.
- Remove and, if needed, replace all dead plants.
- Mow lawn and keep it mowed.
- Trim tree branches near the roofline.

Front yard:

- Cut back to window height all shrubs that block light or the view from windows.
- Move all children's toys to the backyard.
- Clean and sweep paved driveways. Rake, weed, or replenish gravel driveways.

Backyard:

- Remove any extra items from the yard, such as tools, piles of lumber, or auto parts.
- Keep children's toys in one area of the yard. Store them neatly.

APPENDIX E

MOVING CHECKLIST

As a Stager, you can help your clients by sharing this checklist with them. It's another service they will appreciate and will not find elsewhere. Moving takes lots of time and energy, and can be a stressful experience for some people. But with this list, your clients will feel more secure.

SIX WEEKS BEFORE MOVING

- ☐ Make an inventory of everything to be moved.
- ☐ Collect everything not to be moved for a garage sale or charity.
- ☐ Contact the charity for the date/time of pickup. Save receipts for tax records.
- ☐ Contact several moving companies for estimates.
- ☐ Select a mover, arrange for the exact form of payment at the destination (cash, check).

- [ ] Get cartons and packing materials to start packing now.
- [ ] Contact your insurance agent to transfer or cancel coverage.
- [ ] Check with your employer to determine any moving expenses they will pay.

FOUR WEEKS BEFORE MOVING

- [ ] Notify all magazines of your change of address.
- [ ] Check with your veterinarian for pet records and immunizations.
- [ ] Contact utility companies for refunds of deposit; set turnoff dates.
- [ ] Dry-clean clothes to be moved; pack them in protective wrappers.
- [ ] Collect everything you have loaned out; return everything you have borrowed.
- [ ] Service power mowers, boats, snowmobiles, and other such equipment that is to be moved. Drain all gas/oil to prevent a fire in the moving van.
- [ ] Check with your doctors and dentist for all family records and prescriptions.
- [ ] Get your children's school records.
- [ ] Check the freezer and plan to use food over the next two to three weeks.
- [ ] Remove all jewelry and other valuables to a safe deposit box or other safe place to prevent loss during move.
- [ ] Give away or arrange for transportation of houseplants (most moving companies will not move plants).

ONE WEEK BEFORE MOVING

- ☐ Transfer or close checking and savings accounts. Arrange for a cashier's check or money order to pay the moving company upon arrival in your new community.
- ☐ Have your automobile serviced for the trip.
- ☐ Fill out post office change of address forms; give to the local postmaster.
- ☐ Check and make an inventory of all furniture for dents and scratches; notify the moving company of your inventory and compare it to the furniture upon arrival at your new house.
- ☐ Dispose of all combustibles and spray cans (spray cans can explode or burn—don't pack them).
- ☐ Pack a separate carton of cleaning utensils and tools (screwdriver, hammer, etc.).
- ☐ Separate cartons and luggage you need for personal/ family travel.
- ☐ Mark all boxes that you pack with the room they will be going to in your new home.
- ☐ Organize at least one room in the house for packers and movers to work freely.
- ☐ Cancel all newspapers, garden service, and so on.
- ☐ Review the entire list to make certain that you haven't overlooked anything.
- ☐ Check and double-check everything you have done before it's too late.

MOVING DAY

- ☐ Plan to spend the entire day at the house. Last-minute decisions must be made by you.

- ☐ Don't leave until after the movers have gone.
- ☐ Hire a babysitter or send the children to a friend's house for the day.
- ☐ Stay with the moving van driver to oversee the inventory.
- ☐ Tell the packers and/or driver about fragile or precious items.
- ☐ Make a final check of the entire house—basement, closets, shelves, attic, garage, and every room.
- ☐ Approve and sign the bill of lading. If possible, accompany the driver to the weigh station.
- ☐ Double-check with the driver to make certain moving company records show the proper delivery address for your new house. Verify the scheduled delivery date as well.
- ☐ Give the driver your phone numbers both here and in your new community as well as your cell phone number to contact you in case of a problem.
- ☐ Get complete routing information from the driver and phone numbers so you can call the driver or company in case of emergency en route.
- ☐ Disconnect all utilities and advise the agent selling your house that you have done so.
- ☐ Lock all the doors and windows. Advise your real estate agent and neighbors that the house is empty.

APPENDIX F

REGIONAL CHAPTERS FOR THE INTERNATIONAL ASSOCIATION OF HOME STAGING PROFESSIONALS

UNITED STATES

Alabama

Birmingham IAHSP Regional Chapter
birmingham@iahsp.com

Mobile IAHSP Regional Chapter
mobile@iahsp.com

Arizona

Arizona IAHSP Regional Chapter (Phoenix)
azstagingassoc@iahsp.com

Tucson IAHSP Regional Chapter
tucson@iahsp.com

California

Central Valley IAHSP Regional Chapter
centralvalley@iahsp.com

Fresno IAHSP Regional Chapter
fresno@iahsp.com

Greater Sacramento IAHSP Regional Chapter
gssa@iahsp.com

Los Angeles IAHSP Regional Chapter
losangeles@iahsp.com

Marin IAHSP Regional Chapter
marin@iahsp.com

Northern California Foothills IAHSP Regional Chapter
ncafoothills@iahsp.com

Northern Los Angeles IAHSP Regional Chapter
lanorth@iahsp.com

Orange County IAHSP Regional Chapter
orangecounty@iahsp.com

Palm Springs IAHSP Regional Chapter
palmsprings@iahsp.com

Redding IAHSP Regional Chapter
redding@iahsp.com

Redlands IAHSP Regional Chapter
redlands@iahsp.com

San Diego IAHSP Regional Chapter
sandiego@iahsp.com

San Francisco IAHSP Regional Chapter
sanfrancisco@iahsp.com

San Francisco Central Bay Area IAHSP Regional Chapter
sfcbstagingassoc@iahsp.com

San Francisco East Bay Area IAHSP Regional Chapter
ebsa@iahsp.com

San Francisco Peninsula IAHSP Regional Chapter
sfpeninsula@iahsp.com

San Jose IAHSP Regional Chapter
sanjose@iahsp.com

Santa Barbara IAHSP Regional Chapter
santabarbara@iahsp.com

Sonoma County IAHSP Regional Chapter
sonomacounty@iahsp.com

Tracy-Modesto IAHSP Regional Chapter
tracy-modesto@iahsp.com

West Los Angeles IAHSP Regional Chapter
westla@iahsp.com

Colorado

Denver IAHSP Regional Chapter
denver@iahsp.com

Northern Colorado IAHSP Regional Chapter
ncolorado@iahsp.com

Connecticut

Fairfield IAHSP Regional Chapter
connecticut@iahsp.com

Hartford IAHSP Regional Chapter
hartford@iahsp.com

Delaware

Delaware IAHSP Regional Chapter
delaware@iahsp.com

District of Columbia

Washington, DC, IAHSP Regional Chapter
washingtondc@iahsp.com

Florida

Daytona Beach IAHSP Regional Chapter
daytonabeach@iahsp.com

Fort Lauderdale IAHSP Regional Chapter
ftlauderdale@iahsp.com

Jacksonville IAHSP Regional Chapter
jacksonville@iahsp.com

Miami IAHSP Regional Chapter
miami@iahsp.com

Naples IAHSP Regional Chapter
naples@iahsp.com

Northeast Florida IAHSP Regional Chapter
neflorida@iahsp.com

Orlando IAHSP Regional Chapter
cfsa@iahsp.com

South Florida IAHSP Regional Chapter
southflorida@iahsp.com

Tampa Bay IAHSP Regional Chapter
tampabay@iahsp.com

Treasure Coast IAHSP Regional Chapter
treasurecoast@iahsp.com

West Palm Beach IAHSP Regional Chapter
westpalmbeach@iahsp.com

Georgia

Atlanta IAHSP Regional Chapter
atlantastaging@iahsp.com

Atlanta Southern Crescent IRC
southatlanta@iahsp.com

Idaho

Boise IAHSP Regional Chapter
boise@iahsp.com

Illinois

Central Chicago IAHSP Regional Chapter
centralchicago@iahsp.com

Greater Chicago IAHSP Regional Chapter
chicago@iahsp.com

Northeast Illinois IAHSP Regional Chapter
neillinois@iahsp.com

Peoria IAHSP Regional Chapter
peoria@iahsp.com

Southern Illinois IAHSP Regional Chapter
southernillinois@iahsp.com

Indiana

Fort Wayne IAHSP Regional Chapter
fortwayne@iahsp.com

Indianapolis IAHSP Regional Chapter
indianapolis@iahsp.com

Northwest Indiana IAHSP Regional Chapter
nwindiana@iahsp.com

Kansas

Wichita IAHSP Regional Chapter
wichita@iahsp.com

Kentucky

Louisville IAHSP Regional Chapter
louisville@iahsp.com

Northern Kentucky–Greater Cincinnati Ohio, IAHSP
    Regional Chapter
cincinnati@iahsp.com

Paducah IAHSP Regional Chapter
paducah@iahsp.com

Maryland

Annapolis IAHSP Regional Chapter
annapolis@iahsp.com

Central Maryland IAHSP Regional Chapter
centralmaryland@iahsp.com

Harford County IAHSP Regional Chapter
harfordcounty@iahsp.com

Massachusetts

Boston IAHSP Regional Chapter
boston@iahsp.com

Michigan

Ann Arbor IAHSP Regional Chapter
annarbor@iahsp.com

Grand Rapids IAHSP Regional Chapter
grandrapids@iahsp.com

Great Lakes IAHSP Regional Chapter
greatlakes@iahsp.com

Minnesota

Minneapolis/St. Paul IAHSP Regional Chapter
minnstpaul@iahsp.com

Missouri

St. Louis IAHSP Regional Chapter
stlouis@iahsp.com

Nebraska

Omaha IAHSP Regional Chapter
omaha@iahsp.com

Nevada

Las Vegas IAHSP Regional Chapter
lasvegas@iahsp.com

Sierra Nevada IAHSP Regional Chapter
sierranevada@iahsp.com

New Jersey

New Jersey IAHSP Regional Chapter
newjersey@iahsp.com

Northern New Jersey IAHSP Regional Chapter
northernnewjersey@iahsp.com

Southern New Jersey IAHSP Regional Chapter
southnewjersey@iahsp.com

New York

Central New York IAHSP Regional Chapter
centralny@iahsp.com

Long Island IAHSP Regional Chapter
longisland@iahsp.com

New York City IAHSP Regional Chapter
newyork@iahsp.com

Southern New York IAHSP Regional Chapter
southernnewyork@iahsp.com

North Carolina

Charlotte IAHSP Regional Chapter
charlotte@iahsp.com

Raleigh IAHSP Regional Chapter
raleigh@iahsp.com

Ohio

Akron IAHSP Regional Chapter
akron@iahsp.com

Dayton IAHSP Regional Chapter
dayton@iahsp.com

Columbus IAHSP Regional Chapter
columbusohio@iahsp.com

Toledo IAHSP Regional Chapter
toledo@iahsp.com

Oklahoma

Oklahoma City IAHSP Regional Chapter
oklahomacity@iahsp.com

Oregon

Portland IAHSP Regional Chapter
portland@iahsp.com

Pennsylvania

Philadelphia IAHSP Regional Chapter
philadelphia@iahsp.com

Reading Berks IAHSP Regional Chapter
reading@iahsp.com

South Carolina

Greenville IAHSP Regional Chapter
greenville@iahsp.com

Tennessee

Chattanooga IAHSP Regional Chapter
chatanooga@iahsp.com

Nashville IAHSP Regional Chapter
nashville@iahsp.com

Memphis IAHSP Regional Chapter
tennessee@iahsp.com

Texas

Austin IAHSP Regional Chapter
austin@iahsp.com

Dallas IAHSP Regional Chapter
dallas@iahsp.com

Fort Worth IAHSP Regional Chapter
fortworth@iahsp.com

Houston IAHSP Regional Chapter
houston@iahsp.com

San Antonio IAHSP Regional Chapter
sanantonio@iahsp.com

South Central Texas IAHSP Regional Chapter
southcentraltexas@iahsp.com

Utah

Salt Lake City IAHSP Regional Chapter
slc@iahsp.com

Virginia

Hampton IAHSP Regional Chapter
hampton@iahsp.com

Washington

North Puget Sound IAHSP Regional Chapter
npugetsound@iahsp.com

Seattle IAHSP Regional Chapter
seattle@iahsp.com

Tacoma IAHSP Regional Chapter
tacoma@iahsp.com

Vancouver, Washington, IAHSP Regional Chapter
vancouverwashington@iahsp.com

Wisconsin/Minnesota

St. Croix Valley IAHSP Regional Chapter
stcroixvalley@iahsp.com

Wyoming

Cheyenne IAHSP Regional Chapter
cheyenne@iahsp.com

CANADA

Ontario

Aurora Ontario IAHSP Regional Chapter
auroraontario@iahsp.com

Halton Peel IAHSP Regional Chapter
toronto@iahsp.com

London Ontario IAHSP Regional Chapter
londonontario@iahsp.com

Ottawa IAHSP Regional Chapter
ottawa@iahsp.com

HOW TO REACH BARB SCHWARZ

Please visit my web site www.StagedHomes.com.
Or email me at barb@stagedhomes.com.
Or call 1-800-392-7161 or 1-888-277-7824.

INDEX